COFFEE and SYMPATHY

World War II Letters from the Southwest Pacific

April 1943 — January 1945

By

Marcia Ward Behr

Marcia W. Behr

© 2002 by Marcia Ward Behr. All rights reserved.

No part of this book may be reproduced, stored in a retrieval system, or transmitted by any means, electronic, mechanical, photocopying, recording, or otherwise, without written permission from the author.

ISBN: 0-7596-8123-6 (E-book)
ISBN: 0-7596-8124-4 (Paperback)

This book is printed on acid free paper.

1stBooks – rev. 08/15/02

Acknowledgements

I am grateful to my husband, Edward A. Behr, and our son, Edward A. Behr, Jr., and to Glendy Pabst for help in assembling the letters and editing the descriptive sidelights and for the work of artist Ann Holmes who created the map. Also, I am thankful for the support of our son, Robert S. Behr and his family, and for the help and encourgement of Anita Difanis, Richard Krajeck, Mary-Averett Seelye, Faith Jackson, Susan Hartmann of Ohio State University and Joseph Arnold of Johns Hopkins University.

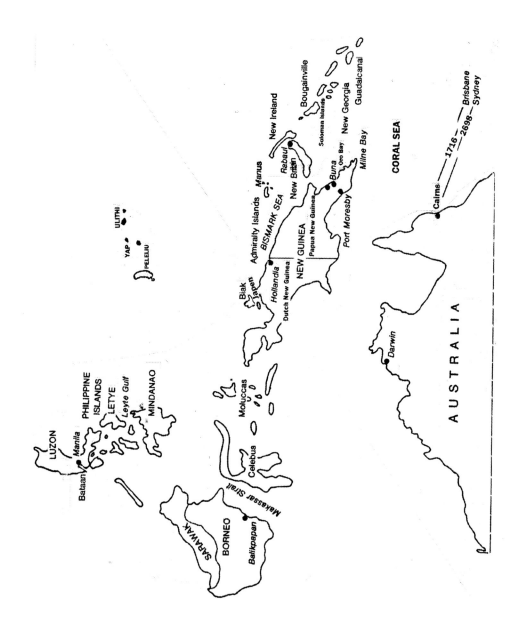

Contents

Acknowledgements iii

Training and Traveling 1

Yorkies Knob 9

Eleanor Roosevelt Slept Here 38

Temptations of the Heart 67

Beachhead Landings 122

Brisbane 126

New Guinea 160

Biak 174

Homecoming 195

About the Author 199

COFFEE and SYMPATHY
World War II Letters from the Southwest Pacific

Training and Traveling

The F.B.I. had investigated me — interviewing neighbors and perhaps suspecting me of radical tendencies as a Bennington College graduate. In the early days of Roosevelt's New Deal, some conservatives were suspicious of students under the influence of very liberal professors. Was I a communist sympathizer? No, certainly not, my friends assured them. So, in late January, 1943, I was cleared to go overseas as a Red Cross recreation worker in World War II.

The Japanese bombed the Navy base at Pearl Harbor on the island of Hawaii, on December 7, 1941. An estimated 1177 men on the battleship Arizona died instantly in that surprise attack. The total killed on the base that infamous day was 2400. At once the United States declared war on the Axis powers (Germany, Italy and Japan). How our country hated the Japanese who immediately seized most of the territories in the Southwest Pacific. The Bataan Death March of our American prisoners on Corregidor in the Philippines only added to the fear and loathing we felt for the Japanese. Americans rallied to help save the world for democracy.

Military supplies in the Pacific were meager at first because the U.S. joined the British in the battle against Hitler's army in Europe and Africa. The Allies were losing the war in the Pacific until we won the crucial naval battles of Midway and Guadalcanal.

By the end of 1942 the American Red Cross was recruiting its own small army of young women to work as staff assistants in combat zones around the world. The requirements for this job were a college-equivalent education and some artistic talent or recreational experience. I had majored in theater and dance and had performed professionally, so was fully qualified.

After signing up I left my family's home in New York City to join a group of new recruits in Washington, D.C. We were housed downtown in several budget hotels. The Ritz where I first lived was next door to a burlesque theatre. But it wasn't sex shows that led the Red Cross to move me and my roommate out of that hotel, it was the mice that ran over our faces at night. Sometimes I simply stood on the bed with the light on until I had to lie down from exhaustion. We did not want to complain for fear the Red Cross would think we were too chicken for duty near battlefronts.

For two months we listened to hours of lectures on the history of the Red Cross and tried to take notes on the talks of male field workers who had been overseas. One day was devoted to learning how to conduct an orchestra and how to inspire servicemen to sing along with the accompaniment of a very simple wind instrument called a tonette. In desperation and with no musical talent whatsoever, I bought a tonette and tried to learn "Home on the Range" and "Keep the Home Fires Burning." I bought books on games, cards, jokes puzzles and magic, I wrote home for the one-act play script of *Sparkin'* by E. P. Conkle, a corny farce that I had played successfully in New York with the Bulgakov Repertory Company.

At last the Red Cross moved me, my roommate and others out of the undesirable quarters into an old house just above Dupont Circle. The place needed renovating and we spent the days scraping and painting our fourth-floor tower-like room. All the time we waited expectantly for secret orders announcing the date and point of departure for overseas duty.

Suddenly, an epidemic of German measles swept through the household. Two of my five roommates and I came down with the three-day disease. I was not very sick, but the doctor had told us to lie in the dark to protect our eyes. So, while the others slept, I had plenty of time to think about everything.

Why had I wanted to join the war overseas? I asked myself. My good friend Pat Rey worked in Washington under General Marshall and learned of the American Red Cross recruitment of women. In fact, she had already signed up. Then she asked me, "Why don't you?" Why not indeed? I was not married and had no real responsibilities. My theatrical career was at a standstill. In fact, I was working for the U.S. Bureau of Censorship scanning civilian mail to and from foreign countries. I even had a picture of me as Jane Doe in a Censorship production encouraging employees to buy U.S. War Bonds.

Then I thought about that good review in the *New York Times* by drama critic Brooks Atkinson, who wrote of my performance in the play *Escape into Glory* — "Marcia Ward knows how to express the hidden torment of a girl who has had a shattering emotional experience." Theatre training can provide skills to overcome real-life moments of "hidden torments." I certainly could laugh and smile through unwelcome inner feelings. I had little knowledge about my future duties, but felt that I could smile through hard tasks, and the brave men fighting the war would appreciate the cheer and sympathy of an American Red Cross woman worker. Yes, it was right to go overseas.

We kept waiting and waiting. What could I write home about my departure? Somehow I assumed we would go to England and wrote home for my old fur coat. In Washington, however, the Red Cross had no idea of when or where we would be traveling or what we would be doing when we got there. Everyone was quite frantic. Every night we ate our last good meal, and every day we bought more soap, Kleenex, stockings and chocolates, said to be unavailable near combat zones.

Troop ships were at a premium, especially on the Atlantic where German submarines were a dangerous presence. At last, however, the Red Cross issued me three tropical uniforms and I sent back the old fur coat. On April 4, 1943, a very excited group of young women boarded a train headed west toward the Pacific Ocean.

Three days later we began an eventful week in San Francisco — cable-car rides, cocktails at the Top of the Mark, dining at Trader Vic's, a trip to the Presidio Army post for a physical checkup, and last minute shopping. Everyone was buying liquor, even non-drinkers, because it might be scarce where we were assigned. I followed suit and purchased an expensive pinch-bottle of Scotch which I knew was something special, even though I had rarely sampled it. I held onto it until I finally gave it to a Navy lieutenant in Australia.

We sailed out of San Francisco on the Army transport, Willard A. Holbrook, a former President Lines ship now bulging with troops. Hearing only rumors about exactly where we were headed, we followed the Equator westward, never seeing a ship, an island or a bird for eighteen days. At last we landed at Southport, Australia, an ocean port down river from Brisbane. Still without receiving specific assignments, we were then sent by train to Sydney, the headquarters city of the American Red Cross.

Now, as I read my letters written so long ago and saved by my mother, I appreciate how daring it was of the American Red Cross to send women overseas to create recreational programs for men close to the war zone. The Red Cross, however, sent us with no apparent understanding of what it might mean to be surrounded by men separated from their wives and sweethearts for months and years. How could they possibly have prepared us for the daily admiration, attention, approval and even romantic overtures of thousands of servicemen at war? Looking back fifty-five years, it seems to me that naivete and guilelessness were a protection to many of us, and at the same time, sometimes did expose us to serious emotional entanglements with the men we came to assist. I would learn about such entanglements later.

Marcia Ward Behr

[on shipboard]
April 30, 1943

Dearest Family,

This is all very amazing. I am now writing from my top berth, and there is a slow roll that I like. Last night the ship was really pitching. We all woke up to hear glasses shattering and strange noises all over — probably people falling out of bed. I hear a great many did. It is marvelous on deck today, warm sun and strong wind, whitecaps galore. Most of the trip, especially near the equator, has been hot and the water smooth and glassy. If I had only known about the clothes we would need on shipboard. I could not stand my grey slacks at all until yesterday. I had to wear my tropical uniform skirt. (The Red Cross had issued me uniforms three sizes too big.) Charlotte Cooper took one in for me and pinned a jacket for me, so I wore a skirt and blouse most of the time.

I had tonsillitis for the first week we were out. I am not sorry, although it was very painful. I could not read because the light was bad. The nights were most unbearable, no air with the portholes closed. A nice doctor took care of me, but it was one of those things that heals by itself regardless of medicines and takes its own sweet time. I had plenty of moments to think.

You can probably guess where we are headed, but that might not be our final destination. There is one place I would like to go in spite of snakes, and another place in spite of filth and smells, but who knows? I have really loved the voyage, even though we have all had our restless moments. There was the night we had to restrain a drunken girl from jumping overboard. My cabin mates are independent souls and we get along well. Our accommodations have been luxurious compared to what I had imagined.

                                               Love,
                                               Marcia

[on shipboard]
April 30, 1943

Dearest Family,

I suppose the most important day of our crossing was the Equator initiation, which eventually turned into a good brawl. I mean by that, it started out in an organized fashion with King Neptune's court presiding. I was the queen decked out in a weird costume, partly Hawaiian and mostly Red Cross, with a crown on my head. A tank of water had been rigged up for the occasion. Pirates with lipstick and black paint and bandanas, looking quite fierce, stood about waiting for the victims.

All officers disliked by their men got the Southern Cross, which, as you may know, is a close shave on their heads in the shape of a cross. Then they were greased, messed up, blindfolded and thrown into the pool. The women were quite roughly treated too, though, thank goodness, no permanent damage. Lots of men got away with very little too. We, in the court, expected to escape initiation, but, in the end someone from above turned on large salt-water hoses, and bedlam rang. Some husky picked me up and threw me into the pool, which was disgustingly dirty by this time, but I just decided what was the use of resisting and had a good time.Such washing and scrubbing afterwards to get ourselves clean. I had to wash my hair, and water was scarce and cold.

I am glad I have some theories to hang onto, because, my Lord, this is quite a war. Even from here I can see that. I would not give up this opportunity for anything, and I feel confident that, if I hang on to what I know, I shall be all right. Do not worry. I realize now that it may be harder for you. I saw that when I got your telegram.

Love,
Marcia

[Sydney]
May 6, 1943

Dearest Family,

I have wanted to write you so much and more often, and now at my tiredest moment I am sitting down to write. I have been traveling ever since Washington and am still traveling. I can tell you that I am in Australia and will stay here. We got our final assignments yesterday, where we shall really start to work. I am very happy about mine.

I think I had better tell you right now before I forget. How I could, I do not know, but I am awfully tired. Yesterday they took newsreel pictures of some girls who have been in New Guinea and some of us were asked to be the background. Imagine our excitement! It is *Pathé News* and will go all over the U. S. The

Marcia Ward Behr

newsmen asked for someone who had done some acting to say a word to the mothers of America — about Mothers' Day — so, I am in the movies! I only say a couple of words. I made them up myself. I felt very honored and proud to have the chance. Do go to the movies and see us. It is supposed to be released soon.

You see everything is so amazing and so much happens at once that you soon begin to take it in your stride. I have thought of you all so much and how you must be worrying about me, but you must not, I am the luckiest girl in the world. I have never eaten such good food in my life — and so much of it.

Washington — Red Cross, I mean — certainly does not know very much about what goes on out here, or they would never have sent us out with the stuff we have. I can get everything except Kleenex. I am glad I brought all my cottons, though I could stand some more pretty things. I don't need any civilian clothes. I think I shall store all my woolens, so the ants won't eat them.

Easter Sunday aboard ship was beautiful. We had sunrise service and I was in the choir. We started just as the sun came up — and it was really moving — no flowers — no pomp and circumstance, but everyone really felt that Christ was risen on Easter. We sang "Christ, the Lord Is Risen Today." The chaplain gave a very simple service, and then we sang the "Alleluia." I managed to stand next to someone who carried the melody strongly, so I sang out safely.

It is winter here, but certainly not cold. The Australians are a happy people. Most of them speak with a semi-cockney accent. I can imitate them quite well. If I don't watch out I won't sound like an American and the boys long to hear an American girl talk once in a while, so I had better keep my hard Rs.

As far as I can see our government is doing a marvelous job over here and appreciated by the Australians, as well as we appreciate them and what they are doing. I really do not know much about it yet.

Give my love to everyone — Muffy, Tom, Sylvia, Nan — Daddy and Mother. I shall write soon again.

Love,
Marcia

[Yorkies Knob]
May 11, 1943

Dearest Family,

Received your letter today with mention of the flow of letters you are awaiting from me. I do not want to disappoint you. It's hard to write letters, you know, when nothing is settled and so much happens, that when nothing happens it is unusual. Right now it is quiet, a short lull, but tomorrow I start traveling again. I am delighted with my assignment. I have heard only good things about the place.

I shall now wash my hair. Everything is clean. I washed and ironed all day. I had supper early and packed. Thank goodness, that's all done. Yesterday I went to the horse races, believe it or not! I felt as though I were at Belmont, though I must say it is a little different. I am very happy and know I shall love my work when I get to the final destination.

I saw the uncut newsreel today. I am easily seen in the group. It will be released in the U. S. in about five or six weeks. Make a habit of going to the movies once a week, if you can afford it.

I still feel close to home. I have to look on a map to realize that I have come all this distance and am sitting where I am. We just finished some Coca-Colas and I am going to bed soon. I have a lot to do tomorrow before night when we start moving again.

Love,
Marcia

[on the train]
May 13, 1943

Dearest Family,

I wonder how you all are. I suppose Tom's and Muffy's wedding is occupying everyone's time and thoughts. I have changed my A.P.O. but the other number will reach me too. They will forward it.

I am writing en route now, so my pen is not steady. Any moment now we shall start a game of bridge which will last for hours. It is really the only way to pass the time. Having been with the same people in close quarters for a couple of months, we are all talked out. I love these trains. They are the European variety and Alfred Hitchcock always uses them as background for his mystery movies. Remember *Night Train*? We are in a compartment for two. I chose the upper berth and I hear that's the best place. Anyway I slept soundly. I can sleep anywhere now.

We stop at stations for our meals. We all get out and go up to the counters where the meat pies with cups of tea are waiting for us. The tea has milk and sugar in it already with tiny ants floating on top. We just skim them off and drink. The train tracks get narrower and narrower as we travel. It takes time to change trains. When the engineer needs a pickup, he simply stops the train and gets out and makes a cup of tea. He squats by the side of the tracks and boils the water in his billy can. We can watch him from the car windows. So you can understand that it takes a long time to travel anywhere.

There are still some things I shall have to conquer, like certain tropical bugs. That will be an accomplishment. I know I am going to be happy in my work and I would not trade places with anyone. I feel so lucky. Do not worry about me. That newsreel is hysterical. My diction sounds so British. I hope I do not sound so affected.

                                                        Love,
                                                        Marcia

COFFEE and SYMPATHY
World War II Letters from the Southwest Pacific

Yorkies Knob

When the American Red Cross headquarters in Sydney told me I was going to Yorkies Knob, they said only that it was a coveted assignment — a club right on the ocean in faraway northern Australia. After a week of steak 'n' eggs, ice cream and shopping, I joined a trainful of Red Cross staff assistants eager to end their six weeks' journey and get on the job.

But what job? I knew only the name of the place in North Queensland. Yorkies Knob, my destination, was just 12 miles up the coast from Cairns, a four-day train ride from Sydney. Red Cross staff workers departed for clubs at various stations along the way: Newcastle, Rockhampton, and Townsville. I imagine those posts were very different from mine, which turned out to be unique indeed. I passed the time playing bridge trying not to imagine the work ahead of me.

I disembarked at Cairns, the northernmost port on the east coast, gateway to the Tablelands and an hour's boat ride to the fantastic Great Barrier Reef. My director, Arlene Carston, an attractive young American about my age, met me in Cairns at the busy Red Cross Club for enlisted men. We had lunch in the pleasant dining room of the former resort hotel which was beautifully situated overlooking the harbor. Then Arlene drove me to my assignment at Yorkies Knob Officers Rest Home.

As soon as I arrived at the club, I felt uneasy because of a visibly tense relationship between Arlene and Helen whose place, it appeared, I was to take. Helen was a forty-year-old Australian woman and very popular with the guest officers. Nevertheless, within a week, she was gone and it was up to me, a twenty-five-year-old, to fill her shoes.

It is impossible to describe in any simple way what my duties were at Yorkies. I remember most of all that there was very little time to myself, just moments snatched when no one needed my attention. Each day Arlene or I drove our pickup truck to Cairns to get supplies: milk and ice cream from the Army commissary, vegetables from the Chinese grocer, bread from the baker, and meat from the butcher. The gas and oil for the truck came from the Quartermaster Corps, and we had to run errands for the help. We planned menus for three meals a day, kept the place clean, ran a weekly dance, gave our guests ready smiles and lots of conversation, played Ping-Pong and darts, pumped the player piano, took walks and swims, or went fishing. Of course, Arlene was in charge and she was sorely tried by four disruptive Filipino workers, who had been lent to us by the Army, as well as by the health problems of the cooks.

When I arrived at Yorkies Knob in late May 1943, we were in a combat area. Soon after the devastating attack on our Navy at Pearl Harbor, December 7, 1941, the United States based the Fifth Air Force at Cairns. Very quickly the Japanese had seized most of the Central and Southwest Pacific islands, as well as the Dutch East Indies, including Dutch New Guinea and key bases along the coast of Australian-mandated Papua New Guinea. Only Port Moresby, on the southern Papuan coast, remained under the Australian control. It was just a few hundred miles north of Cairns and crucial to the defense of Australia itself. The war in the Pacific was going sadly for the Allies until they achieved two great victories. First we won the naval battle of Midway in June 1942, providing an emotional lift for the United States. Then in October came the naval success off Guadalcanal Island, beginning the offensive against Japan.

However, it took six long months of savage fighting, from August 1942 to February 1943, to drive out the Japanese from the Guadalcanal jungle. The Australians never did lose control of Port Moresby and the Allies had gained Milne Bay, Buna and Guadalcanal. Australia was saved.

Even before the end of the Guadalcanal struggle, the Red Cross began in late 1942 to renovate the two-story hotel at Yorkies Knob and turn it into a charming officers rest home. The hotel had been a notorious bar and brothel and there were rumors of botched abortions. Yet it was beautifully situated right on the ocean. In peacetime, tourists came to Cairns to visit the magical Great Barrier Reef, and to take inland excursions to the Tablelands. This was 600,000 acres of highland with fertile fields, orchards, forests, clear streams and waterfalls, and deep blue peaks and ranges that paled to grey in the distance.

The Fifth Air Force, based at Cairns, protected Port Moresby in New Guinea from seizure by the Japanese and helped to stave off the threatened invasion of Australia, Between missions the pilots enjoyed coming to Yorkies Knob. One young married officer fell in love with Elaine White, the Australian secretary. When there was no longer the threat of a Japanese invasion, in the early spring of 1943, the Fifth Air Force pulled out of Cairns taking along Elaine's pilot, and she never recovered from the loss. She finally went home to Melbourne. This sad story aroused my sympathy, but I do not remember thinking that it could happen to me, beware.

Yorkies Knob was romantic especially at night. Through the palm trees we watched the moon's shimmering path over the ocean and in the pale light we could see the wild orchids on the branches. Bougainvillea and poinsettia grew everywhere and we could always faintly smell the sweet frangipani blossoms. The only other dwellings facing the wide stretch of white sand were a few humble cottages now empty. The broad white beach continued for miles, but ended abruptly at the knob-like hill beside the hotel. The knob rose steeply from both ocean and hotel, and the slope was covered with mango trees. When the sweet juicy-fruit ripened, chattering flying foxes came to devour them. Sometimes wallabies wandered down onto the shore.

The men, up to 20 at a time, slept at one end of the two-story club. At the other end was the porch where Arlene and I each had cubicles. In the middle was a long, narrow sitting room with several windows that looked out on the ocean. The secretary slept in a room back of our porch. There were no screens, only decorative latticework. The Aussies believed screens would keep out the air.

The dining room could seat over 100 people in two shifts. There were two wood-burning stoves in the kitchen and next to it a storeroom with hooks for hams. A cumbersome, old-fashioned icebox had been rescued from an antiquated truck and placed outside on the patio. Blocks of ice were delivered irregularly; or we often had to fetch them ourselves from town. A modest building served for a ballroom and it held a Ping-Pong table, dart board, and a player piano. When the piano was loaded with a roll of music, someone pumped it with his feet, while the rest of us gathered around and sang at the tops of our lungs.

There was little indoor plumbing — cold running water in the kitchen and at a few sinks plus a crude shower on the patio out back. Our electric generator ran a pump to bring sun-warmed water from a tank nearby. That was fine for a shower, but water had to be heated for dishwashing. The privies were several yards behind the hotel. At night we turned our flashlights in every direction to make sure there were no rats or snakes. The privies actually hung over a swampy area, and inside there were plenty of spiders, tarantulas, and various tropical insects to face. I hated to go there at night. The doors of the rest home had no locks. The only bad guys were our enemies, the Japanese, and we girls felt completely safe. The terms "sexual abuse" and "sexual harassment" were not in anyone's vocabulary. Rape, yes. However, most women and men took the then-prevalent moral code seriously. We believed that men would respect us and we enjoyed their admiration and friendship.

Only once did I feel it necessary to insist vehemently I was a "good girl." The officer in question had never been to Yorkies before. I was on duty alone and he was the only overnight guest. We had exhausted the Pianola and the Ping-Pong playing. Suddenly his mood changed and he said something that I did not quite understand. He didn't make any physical gesture toward me, but I guessed what he meant. My tears finally persuaded the officer to stop and he left. The next morning he apologized profusely.

Naturally, I had not foreseen such awkward moments when I came to Yorkies. Nor had I envisioned my romance with a Navy lieutenant whom I met at Yorkies Knob. On October 20, 1943, a Navy LST docked at Cairns to take on supplies before sailing north to the New Guinea war zone. Lieutenant Jim Wilder and three other officers from the ship came out to Yorkies Knob to have dinner and swim. They had such a good time that they returned the next day and stayed for our weekly dance. I agreed to write to Jim, little foreseeing any important consequences.

From the beginning of the war Cairns had been designated a combat zone. Ships of all kinds moved in and out of the harbor on their way to and from the New Guinea area. Cairns was an important Navy supply base. The Fifth Air Force had gone, but the Amphibious Engineers were maneuvering and practicing island landing skills.

American Red Cross Clubs had been in the Pacific area since early 1942. At first Australians had been recruited to operate the clubs, while the Red Cross in Washington trained young women to replace the Australians in the growing number of overseas clubs. By 1943 large enlisted men's clubs all over the world provided accommodations and activities for thousands of American soldiers, sailors, Marines and airmen.

Rest homes for G.I.s and officers were sprinkled about Australia, New Zealand and New Caledonia, a French territory 1,000 miles off the east coast of Australia. They offered a quiet break away from the rigors of the battlefront. Yorkies Knob Officers Rest Home provided an escape for Allied personnel on leave and for those awaiting battle assignments.

[Yorkies Knob]
May 22, 1943

Dearest Family,

I have not written for a week. Now I am writing from the spot where I expect to be for some time. Nothing is as I imagined it.

The work is easy and yet the most difficult job that I could ever have dreamed. Naturally, I still have not acclimated myself and feel a little shy. I think I have bumped into something that will eventually straighten out. I felt a lack of harmony in our small organization when I came, and I thought it must have something to do with my butting in, through no fault of mine. However, this discord has been coursing for sometime. I feel, though I say nothing, that there really is no cause or need for trouble. When I hear about it from both sides, it sounds quite inconsequential. Nevertheless, coming into a sort of smothered uneasiness, and meeting twenty-five or more new people a day, is a slight strain, you must admit. I will not for a moment stop to wonder or pity myself, because I know that eventually, when I feel at home here, I shall relax and be able to react spontaneously.

I tell you all this not to have you believe that I am at all unhappy. It is not that things are happening inside of me to make me miserable, but that, for a time, it is hard for me to adjust to the intangibility of the job.

I wish I could express myself more neatly, but I do not want to make any mistakes in what I say. You know what I am like when I have stage fright before a performance — well, I am a little bit like that now and waiting for the curtain to go up. I am only hitting on one side of my personality and I keep searching for the rest of me. This whole process is a personality game and I think being conscious of that is a strain.

Yorkies Knob is a perfectly delightful place. It is an officers' rest home, and I have met so many nice people. Naturally, they all observe a newcomer and you may rest assured that I am conscious of that. It is up to me to work out my own routine, as far as work around the club is concerned, but at the same time to take orders and ask questions. Since there are so very few on the staff here, we must be on duty most of the time. I do not mind.

Of course, being an American girl fresh from the States, I have been asked out, but it is better to stick close to home for a while and observe than to leave my responsibilities too often. At any rate, that is not why I came over here. Each day I relax a little more, and yesterday was almost fun. I was here at the club all day. There were not many people around and those that were here entertained themselves and me too. We did very simple things — looking at the fish trap, riding around in funny little cars over bumpy roads, picked flowers and ate. The food is very good — plain but well cooked (an excellent lemon meringue pie, almost as good as yours, Mother.)

In the evening I went to a dance with a very nice officer. We had a nice long talk on the way back, and he gave me some welcome advice. He understood my feelings about coming into this situation and I felt better about the whole thing. The dance was lots of fun. I was really the belle of the ball.

Don't worry about me. I could not be in better surroundings.

Love and kisses,
Marcia

Marcia Ward Behr

[Yorkies Knob]
May 26, 1943

Dearest Family,

I am in town doing the shopping today. Little did I know my job would partly consist of running an inn. I was scared at first because it meant telling other people what to do, as much as anything and then seeing that they did it. Arlene, my club director, is going on leave some time soon, for a couple of weeks. That is going to be something! I think we shall get along very well. We have an excellent cook, and a girl who helps her and five Filipinos (lent by the Army to the Red Cross) who are apt to be temperamental, but so far I have not had any trouble with them. In fact, they amuse me and I am quite fond of them. Then there is another woman, a good and thorough worker who is coming to help upstairs. So you see it is easy. The only thing is to keep peace in the house, and I just do not expect any discord.

I have some pictures I want to send you. Perhaps they will give you some idea. Don't for a moment worry about me or pity me, I am living in comparative luxury. Of course, it is not home and I miss you all dreadfully, but I would not have missed this opportunity for the world. I only hope I can make people happy enough, so I shall not have come in vain. I feel more at home now and I have met hundreds of nice people. This job is teaching me how to get on and talk to all kinds, men especially. Instead of liking or disliking a person at once, I look for something good about them and finesse what I would ordinarily consider discouraging factors in an individual.

                                              Love and kisses to everyone,
                                              Marcia

[Yorkies Knob]
May 28, 1943

Dearest Family,

I must hurry and make my bed and see that the other beds get made.

A couple of days ago I started this letter hoping to get it finished before Arlene went to town.

I am in charge of the upstairs work. I have been told by everyone that the Filipinos are difficult. You tell them to do something and you must check up on

COFFEE and SYMPATHY
World War II Letters from the Southwest Pacific

them and tell them to do it again and again. I was really worried because I hate to give people orders, especially when I expect them to talk back and not obey. When I first arrived our upstairs boy, Marceleno, was in the brig for disobedience. He has been back just a few days now. There is one old Filipino who is a darling. He is Ramon and has no teeth and you can barely understand him, but he is willing to do anything. We tell him what we want the others to do and he gives the orders.

Well, the first day Marceleno was back I had to give him orders. So far I have had no trouble whatsoever. He seems to have a very good disposition and obeys me. Arlene wanted the window sills washed. I came up while he was washing them and he remarked about the dirt and then I noticed that the window panes were in need of cleaning too. We both laughed and I said, "Well, that is for another day." This morning I saw that the window panes were clean.

One of the Filipinos is a little bit sullen and does not smile much, but I just do not expect them to be disagreeable and so far they have been very good. There are three young boys and Ramon. Naturally, they do not like this work. They have probably not done it before, and they are far away from their homeland. If they but realized it, this is a soft job, plenty of Army money and lots of free time.

The first thing I was told is that shopping for food is difficult and that it can be a job getting certain supplies. However, if people have the goods to give, I have found them willing to help. There are lots of headaches with this place, especially keeping employees — good cooks and a man for the outside.

Arlene is a young girl and has the responsibility of Yorkies. She came at Christmastime after some Australians had opened the club. I found that I was the so-called successor to a very popular Australian woman about forty-five. Many of the boys have said, "She makes the club." Apparently, she and Arlene did not jibe and Arlene finally got rid of her. I don't know the whole story. Helen seems nice and may have faults. At any rate, I certainly walked into a personality setup. I just try to be pleasant and do the right thing.

Tomorrow I have been asked to go for a long drive in the country and that pleases me. It is supposed to be a beautiful trip and I shall be gone all day. It is my first day off since I have been here and it will probably do me lots of good to get away. A very nice captain asked me. He and some others go every Friday to test the milk. I planted some flowers the other day and they are showing signs of life. We have three wee chicks and hope to have chicken some day. I have not had any in Australia. We have lots of milk and eggs, though, and butter, steaks and fresh vegetables and ice cream, so do not pity me. I live in the lap of luxury. I heard rats last night and the toads are big, but I am getting used to them, not the rats though.

Marcia Ward Behr

I have to go to town to shop now. We are twelve miles away. I would write more often, but it is hard. Not that I do much, but I have to be around all the time with the guests. Last night was dance night again.

I hope you like the pictures. If I get any more, I'll send them.

Lots of love to all,
Marcia

[Yorkies Knob]
June 1, 1943

Dearest Family,

What a joy to receive all your letters. I have only received V-mail before, but yesterday I got ten letters, one from Tom and one from Daddy. Some of them were written before you heard from San Francisco. It made me shed a tear to think you were so worried about me. Of course, I never thought about myself. It certainly is easier for the person going than the ones left behind. I'll bet you were really glad I went on the Pacific. The war will probably last longer over here, but I do not feel very far away from you. Your letters are so vivid. It is the next best thing to being there, but I would hate to miss this experience. Of course, Australia is not as interesting, quaint or Old World as Africa, India, China or England. However, I am probably in a healthier, cleaner climate and country and getting more food than I would anywhere else. The need to take care of the boys is equal all over the world and who knows where I might be sent from here. If the men go, we go.

Yesterday a boy in the Navy called me. I met him when I was in headquarters city over here. He came out to Yorkies Knob with some friends for dinner. They were all so nice and such fun. I have to go on a short trip now, just for the day. Will write more later.

Love to all,
Marcia

COFFEE and SYMPATHY
World War II Letters from the Southwest Pacific

[Yorkies Knob]
June 12, 1943

Dearest Family,

You would laugh to see how popular I am, and how tired I get of it sometimes. You know me, how I used to be. Some people I could just not stand, well now I must like them all, and I do. It is a game with me. I only hope I do not meet someone I really like, because it is much easier this way.

This is the first time this week that I have had a moment, and I should not be writing now, I suppose, but our guests seem to be happy and amusing themselves, so it is all right.

We had two Navy boys here this week. They stayed three nights. They were both lots of fun. We laughed and laughed. They were crazy but fun. Since we are over twelve miles from town, transportation out here is sometimes difficult. These two got a couple of nags and started out on horseback. The horses were so thin and old and hungry that they got a hundred yards and then stopped dead from exhaustion and malnutrition, and they had to pull them back. I finally picked them up after shopping and brought them to the Knob.

They loved it here. I believe we have the best food around and though it is quiet and there is not much to do, except simple pleasures — outdoor sports, Ping-Pong, sleeping. I think people love to come here and relax.

I got a letter yesterday from a boy I met on the ship and he said he saw me in the newsreel. Yesterday an Air Corps pilot arrived who said he had seen me in the newsreel and that it was very good. I do hope you see it some day.

Daddy tells me that the wedding is to be the third of July. Oh, happy day! Something unusual in the Ward family. I am glad it is the oldest first, but I doubt that it will follow accordingly. I can conceive the possibility, but I think it would be more than advisable to await the end of the war. There might be a risk under these conditions. At any rate, I thought we were not supposed to, but I just heard of two Red Cross girls who married enlisted men, no less. In Washington any mere acquaintance with the like was taboo. Which is silly. All our work is for them for the most part and therefore we should be able to use our own discretion. Out here I do not have that trouble because it is for officers only.

Arlene goes on her leave next week and I shall be in charge for two weeks. Elaine White, the nice Australian girl, will help me but, oh boy, I am going to have to keep on my toes. I think we shall all be happy here.

Love,
Marcia

Marcia Ward Behr

[Yorkies Knob]
June 13, 1943

Dearest Family,

We are going to have some help to fix up the fish trap again, so we can have fish. We always used to get plenty every day. It seems you are supposed to have a license for a piece of beach and water, and some old man came along and said the license had not been paid by us, so he bought it.

One day one of the Filipinos came back with an empty bag and said that an old lady with long hair and a dog were getting fish out of the trap, and that we could not use it. Then this old thing, who was really an old man, changed the shape of the trap, so that he did not get any fish at all. So, finally, after several tides had come and gone and no fish, he went away and took all the wire netting with him.

Now, today we are fortunate in getting it fixed up again and once more we shall have fish: mud and sand crab, crayfish (like lobster), king salmon and barimundi, black brim, silver brim, grunter, cod, grey snapper, butterfish, mullet, flathead, and flounder last but not least. That's quite an assortment. Meat is much easier to buy around here than fish, so we are lucky to have a fish trap.

I met a boy in town yesterday who came over on the ship with me. At first I could not remember where I had seen him. He is the only one who has come this way. I have no idea what happened to all the others. Probably all up north somewhere.

Give my love to Nan, Syl, Tom and Muffy and you and Dad,
Marcia

[Yorkies Knob]
June 16, 1943

Dearest Family,

Here is a picture one of the officers took of us three girls. You can see we are all very happy. I really feel very lucky having been assigned to this place. Probably I would have liked any place they sent me, but this seems better than most I have seen.

COFFEE and SYMPATHY
World War II Letters from the Southwest Pacific

It is now June 20. Thursday Arlene left for a two-week leave and I became the head woman. I have had no trouble so far. It is fun planning the meals and going shopping. I am always as nice as I can be to the shopkeepers and we have pleasant chats, so that sometimes I am able to get certain foods that are rare. I wish I could get hold of some celery and we could have a good chicken salad. Just for fun I'll tell you the menus for last night and today.

Last night's supper: tomato juice, pork chops, fried cauliflower in bread crumbs, string beans (like yours, French style), scalloped potatoes and chocolate pudding with stiff egg whites on top. Sunday breakfast: pawpaw, whole-wheat cereal, eggs and bacon. Lunch: pineapple juice, roast chicken, good green peas, Harvard beets, mashed potatoes, ice cream and chocolate sauce. Supper: tomato juice, spaghetti and meatballs, ice cream and butterscotch sauce.

Isn't your mouth watering? And am I getting fat! I am going to start reducing or get some violent exercise like riding a bicycle. Don't you think the meals well balanced? Have you any suggestions?

This morning I had a little problem with the help. Nobody wants to be detailed to wipe the dishes, and since we have four Filipinos besides the Australians working, someone should do it. The Filipinos, like children, try to get out of as much work as possible.

Last night we had a bang-up business for dinner at the last moment, lots of brass hats including a general. Arlene would be away now. We have to take inventory this week and I just got a letter from the Red Cross asking for weekly reports of my successful programs. How can I have programs, when I am shopping all day, and trying to run the house somehow? Here I am a little staff assistant turned club director.

I went to an Australian dance on Friday night. It was very amusing. They do a number of country dances, and always take the girls back to their seats after each dance. I'll mail this and write more later.

Love,
Marcia

[Yorkies Knob]
June 22, 1943

Dearest Family,

Today seemed one of those days that everything was "out of key." We tried some new ideas for lunch. I wanted some cream of corn soup, like yours, with

Marcia Ward Behr

onions. When it came on the table it was lukewarm, which never happens, and greasy. I suppose too much butter cooked with the onions. Then I said cold cuts, but we got scrambled eggs with ham and parsley, and a cheese and rice dish that was not good. The bread seemed moldy and the milk turning. The baked apples were good, but the sauce had curdled. Oh, well! I just hoped no one else had as sour a taste as I did.

We have had some awfully nice Navy boys here, two of them we know very well. They feel they are one of the family. In fact that is the way all feel who stay here, or who come often for meals and visits. Lt. Charles Latus, of Rockville Center, Long Island, I met in Sydney. He brought me some local newspapers yesterday. The other is Ensign John Billie from Bayonne, New Jersey. They are both very natural and lots of fun.

Tomorrow night is Wednesday, our dance night. We have had to change orchestras and now we are going to have a 12-piece orchestra. I don't know how we shall have room to dance, and the noise will probably blast us out, but it is an excellent band, all former professionals, so it ought to be a good dance. We are getting some extra girls from town, so I hope everything is all right. The nights are none too warm now, so I think we shall serve coffee as well as milk.

Arlene certainly went away at a good time. Red Cross headquarters has a new program director who wants a weekly report of our programs and an inventory. I am now the only one who drives, and that means a daily bumpy ride in and out of town. Everything closes at noon, so you may have to stay for lunch. I do like shopping, though, but each little errand takes a long time and you cannot hurry the shopkeepers.

Nan's letter was excellent. Congratulations to her for being elected president of her class and getting the summer job at Stern's. Tom and Muffy will be married when you get this. I shall send a cable. I shed a tear thinking about the wedding and wish I could be there, but I am not unhappy here. This is unbelievable work and I like it more and more.

Love,
Marcia

[Yorkies Knob]
July, 4, 1943

Dearest Family,

Yesterday I received five more letters with newspaper clippings — wonderful stage news, and Nan's letter. I got the one about the new postal system. I shall number them New York 28 now. Honestly, I have written lots of letters to you and in detail. I wish I could tell you where I am, but that is impossible. It is a beautiful place and those pictures that I sent are the murals in our little dance hall painted by a paratrooper who visited once.

The first week with Arlene away was a strain. I probably took everything too seriously, but can you blame me? I used to hate to go buy a pound of hamburger, or call to make an appointment, but here I was, boss of the establishment. Of course, it seemed to me everything happened to me. The power plant went flooey and we had to use a temporary engine. Just before Arlene left she said the whole place had to be inventoried, including all the stuff that is in the cottages where the help lives. The orchestra that we have for the Wednesday night dances is too busy and cannot come any more. It was up to me to get some other band. I was scared of being in charge of dance night anyway.

I had to think up menus every day and get the supplies from town; I could not be here to see what was going on. Elaine White was working on accounts and in charge of the inventory and she could not do much to help me. I simply did not stop to think how I was going to get by the two weeks, but just what had to be done and then do it.

It's now July 5, Monday morning. After lunch yesterday there were lots of people around and I was busy talking to everyone and playing Ping-Pong. I am getting so good at the game, but then, I get a lot of practice.

For the dance last Wednesday, I was fortunate in getting one of the Army orchestras, a twelve-piece band — all of them professional — and a singer who used to be with Glenn Miller.

I thought about you all day July 3rd. I wondered what you were doing every minute. I'll bet Tom was the typical nervous groom. Did you have champagne? Did Muffy look absolutely beautiful, and Syl and Nan? I had some good champagne Sat. night. That's the first bit I have had in Australia, and they do have good wines here. It just happened that a Navy boy found the bottle in a little town and gave it to some civilians who had been nice to him, and they asked us over to help them drink it. I drank to Tom and Muffy.

                                                                    Love,
                                                                    Marcia

Marcia Ward Behr

[Yorkies Knob]
July 5, 1943

Dearest Family,

I am writing on a *Time* magazine dated May 24, our latest, so you see we do get the news eventually. Then our daily newspaper probably has as much war news as you have, though the articles are brief and to the point. The front page is entirely devoted to advertising and the employment situation. You look then at the inside page for the headline news. I loved reading the clippings you sent, thank you.

Your letters give such vivid pictures of all of you and your daily happenings. Sometimes I laugh right out loud especially about Daddy and the lobsters. He knows how to get the most out of them.

I was going to tell you about the dance. Well, as I said, I got this twelve-piece orchestra and the first Wednesday after Arlene left, Elaine and I thought it would be nice to have some extra girls from town for some of the boys who do not know many. Mrs. Darley, whose husband is manager of a bank, said she could get about ten for us. Then, Wednesday morning she called to say that none of the girls could come, but that they would come the next week. There was nothing I could do but hope the usual crowd of officers would come and bring dates and that somehow the dance would be a success.

Ever since I have been here I would not say that the dances have been good mainly because the little five-piece orchestra we had was not very wonderful. In fact, I used to dread the evening, although I was always danced with, but still I did not think everyone was having a nice time. You see, naturally, there is no drinking in Red Cross clubs and some people just do not have fun without it, so that keeps people away too.

Well, it was an awfully cold night and at nine o'clock there were only a few couples there. The orchestra was marvelous, but not many people came and the orchestra left at eleven. I was glad the night was over and knew something would have to be done about the next dance.

Mrs. Darley was our hope. We had a super orchestra and we just needed girls. Mrs. Darley promised they would come, and I invited them for dinner and thought I would give them fillet. It is really steak and pronounced the way it looks.

Tuesday afternoon a Lieutenant in the Army called up to ask if he could give a party for 20 or so in honor of Miss Thompson who was head of the Red Cross service club in town, and is now supervisor of this whole district. We said yes, of course and, since he wanted to come on dance night too, we decided not to have fillet because we couldn't get enough for 110 people. Having so many people meant two sittings in the dining room, because it only seats 54.

The dining room is more a rectangle than a square. The walls are yellow and the tables which seat six people are a soft green color. There are yellow poles, holding up the house really. Lt. Hillman wanted the tables set in an L shape. Elaine and two of the Filipinos and I spent about an hour trying to figure out how we could fix the tables and avoid the poles, so that people would not have to talk to each other around them. It was impossible, so we strung five tables down the middle and put one the other way making a distorted T shape.

The lieutenant came in the afternoon bearing a slew of various flowers and pretty colored leaves. He had never been out here before, and I think he rather expected a luxurious country inn affair, where one throws a big banquet every night. He got a slight shock. He comes from New York City and talks like a big promoter. He said he puts on banquets at the Astor.

I said to him, "I suppose you want white table clothes?" He answered, "Of course." (We use homemade green linen fringed mats.) He planned to bring the tablecloths with him and to arrive just a little before dinner, so we could then set the tables.

Lieutenant Hillman was worried about getting the tables reset and decorated in time, and so was I but I told him not to worry. He wanted four Filipinos to wait on the tables. We usually use two for the whole dining room and, at that, they are so fast you have to hold on to the plate if you want to finish everything. However, we said he could have three, one just to pour the coffee. Then he wanted to tip the three Filipinos ten shillings a piece. I said you will have to tip the other five who will have as much extra work to do behind scenes. The cooks and the upstairs worker are all excited and working harder for the party; besides they do not need tips for an inspiration. They love crowds and the excitement of a party is enough. He went away a little apprehensive about the whole thing. I was too.

Mrs. Darley called and said she had seventeen girls (from local families) coming for dinner. I had done nothing about getting enough men for dinner, because usually a lot come anyway, but this night only one or two had made reservations. I thought, perhaps, there would not be enough men for the dance and how awful that would be. I wanted the girls at 6:30 sharp and, as we had so few men guests for dinner, we did not need to use the lieutenant's tables after all.

I spent two hours arranging the flowers in the dining room. I knew Lt. Hillman wanted all the flowers in a floral drape on his tables, but I thought it best to make the whole room look pretty and have flowers on all the tables and on the buffets. It really did look pretty when I finished. I put small vases of little pink and purple blossoms on the tables and the colored leaves and poinsettias and big fruit baskets on the side tables. We set up the other tables for the girls and left the long tables for the white cloths.

The girls had not come yet and it was a few minutes before seven. I was on the edge of my seat waiting for those white tablecloths, so we could set up for the lieutenant's party before Mrs. Darley and the girls arrived. I decided to heck with the white ones and set all of his tables with the green mats. I worked fast and the Filipinos helped me. We do not have enough teacups with handles, but Miss Thompson had loaned me some from her club in town. We had to change and put all the good cups and glasses on the lieutenant's tables. I did not stop to think that my guests would suffer, but just wanted to make the lieutenant happy, even without white table cloths.

Mrs. Darley and the girls arrived, very attractive girls, and I was just finishing setting-up. The dinner gong did not ring right away, meanwhile some of the lieutenant's guests arrived and I had to greet them since he was not here yet. Mrs. Darley and the girls finally sat down. I had pineapple juice, veal, beans, cauliflower, mashed potatoes and brown betty. As I was eating the mashed potatoes and making polite conversation with Mrs. Darley, Lt. Hillman arrived with his arms full of white table cloths. His mouth opened as he saw the tables all set up. I jumped up and explained that I just could not wait. He understood and I went back to my seat while he put place cards around. In between veal and dessert I heard the orchestra arrive and tune up and I needed chairs for them. I could not give them any until we had finished eating or until enough people got up, so I could use some dining room chairs.

However, my worries were unnecessary, because I found a number of officers had arrived and, when the girls left the tables at 7:45, they went right out and started dancing, so that the dance started an hour earlier than usual. The orchestra was in rare form and this time they brought the sergeant who used to sing with Glenn Miller.

The dance was a huge success. I almost forgot to break for coffee and milk. Mrs. Darley told me the girls were all dying to come again. Lt. Hillman was pleased as punch with his dinner party. The three Filipinos stood around and applauded each speaker and one of them spilled a tray of silver just at the appropriate moment during a dull speech.

                                                        Love,
                                                        Marcia

COFFEE and SYMPATHY
World War II Letters from the Southwest Pacific

[Yorkies Knob]
July 18, 1943

Dear Aunt Mary,

I am very lucky to have been given my present assignment. We are surrounded by tropical beauty, palm trees and tree orchids in our front yard. I never cease to admire the lovely shrubs with their bright-colored leaves and the poinsettias practically growing wild. To think we cherish a small plant with one flower at Christmas time. It is good I landed here in the winter, though, because it is not really cold, and I know it will be steaming hot in the summer.

I have noticed differences in the fruits and vegetables. The sweet potatoes over here are so big, one would be enough for a small family dinner. The carrots seem more like a cross between squash and yams. The native grapefruit is pretty sour, but their oranges are sweeter than ours. The celery is green, though it tastes the same. The radishes seem stronger and the milk much richer. I suppose all the cream goes into it.

I had a wonderful ocean voyage to get here. No rough seas and no war worries. Except for the inconveniences of war travel, such as no hot water and crowded quarters, it was like a South Sea Island cruise. We sailed along the line of the equator, and it was hot at night with the portholes closed, but the food was good and plenty of it.

Next time I shall not be so slow in writing.

Love,
Marcia

[Yorkies Knob]
July 19, 1943

Dearest Family,

Arlene just called from town to say I have a big, fat letter from you. Someone has just arrived for lunch so I'll finish this later.

After lunch I took a walk down the beach by myself and decided to get a little sun. I put on my shorts and a halter which I made out of a scarf I found in town — took a Time magazine and a pillow. While I was there a couple of Navy boys came to look at the water — testing the bottom for our prospective shark net. We hope to have one pretty soon with the help of the military. So far, no shark casualties, though we did see one quite close to shore the other day. We only dip our fannies now, and I have only been swimming once since coming here.

We do have our problems. I told you about the fish trap. Well, a detail came and fixed it up again but Mr. Buckley, a native, says it still won't catch any fish. One of our guests, who used to be here quite often and came back for a visit, went out to try and fix it today. He says he originally helped build it.

We generate our own electricity and hope and prey the lights last through each evening. They just went on now. The noise from the engine is quite deafening but we are so used to it, we hardly notice it penetrating the stillness now. We requisitioned a new engine from headquarters which ought to be here any time within the next year. However, we have Aladdin lamps in reserve and they give almost as much light as an electric lamp. Two new refrigerators came. They will help a lot, if we ever get them installed. It will be good to get rid of the old truck icebox.

Arlene is now working on Septic tanks or skeptic tanks as I call them. She keeps right after them and persistency is what counts.

Yesterday I took a beautiful ride. It was nice to get away and see some of the countryside. My newsreel picture was in town last week. Lots of people saw it. It may have been an Australian release only, but I do hope you get a chance to see it. I have seen a couple of movies over here but they were very bad and I slept through both of them.

Is Sylvia almost a barrister by now? Does she like working in a law office? Nan will be a buyer at Stern's soon and Tom in his own office, imagine! How is Dad's law business? I hope good.

Love,
Marcia

[Yorkies Knob]
July 23, 1943

Dearest Family,

You ask if I am happy to be here. Everyone asks me that all the time and how I happened to join the Red Cross, anyway. You know me. I think I have always wanted to be doing something that has some value to myself or other people.

There are naturally off-moments when I feel a little bit lonely and wonder if I am doing much, but that soon passes.

Arlene is going to town soon and I would like her to mail this. Mrs. Hayhoe, who cleans upstairs, is away taking her daughter to school, and we expect a number of guests this weekend, so I shall have to get busy. Though I was in bed at 11:30 last night, it was very chilly this morning and I hated to get up early.

Yesterday we had an offer of some chickens. We can keep them in the backyard and then always have them when we want chicken for dinner.

I bought some things in a little town I visited on Thursday, some makeup, a slip for a present, some funny rayon underwear, a blouse which I lost, and some other oddities. We had supper at a little place by a waterfall, and had a boiled dinner with cabbage and custard. The old lady who owns the place gave me a flitch of bacon and some fruitcake. It was awfully cold coming home and I was glad to get into bed under five blankets. Arlene is going now.

> Much love,
> Marcia

[Yorkies Knob]
July 26, 1943

Dearest Family,

I have been waiting around all morning to go into town. I always like to get off early and get back in time for lunch. I really do not like eating any place but here at Yorkies Knob. There is no place in town to eat except the Red Cross Club.

Just as I started this letter Arlene called me. I had to go. I was waiting until the hired hand, who ruined our water pump and messed up our engine that runs the electricity, had packed his stuff in the back of the car. Arlene finally was able to get someone to come out here for two weeks to repair the damages and teach old Ramon how to run the machines. He will do a better job than Bert because he won't fuss with them all the time, and keep turning the engine on and off just to see if it works, and hoping it doesn't, so he can fix it again. He lived in a tent in back of the place, and it certainly was a mess to clean up after he left.

Of course, we do not understand these mechanical things, but we do know that when there isn't any water something has to be done. We are using the cistern water now and hoping to get the pump working again very soon.

Elaine Chapman sent me a letter with a newspaper picture in it which I am enclosing. It was taken when I first landed in Australia.

When I read that news about Leo Bulgakov in the movie *For Whom the Bell Tolls,* I just screamed out loud for joy. I am so glad for them. I do hope he gets other parts. They deserve some security, as well as recognition. He has lots of faults, but he has artistry and that's what counts. I do hope I can see the picture some day. I'll bet it is a good one. If it had not been for Franco, it would have been released before I left and I could have seen it. Another reason why fascism should be stopped.

The war news is good, isn't it? Wonder where Mussolini is hiding. Maybe, it won't be such a long time before I see you all again.

So Pat Rey is in England. I wonder where Mary Jeff Wells is? I must write to Pat. In a way I envy her, although I am terribly lucky to be where I am. We are probably better fed than anybody in the world, including the U. S. From what I read about the food situation in Time magazine, I worry about you. I suppose you manage, but it isn't a bed of roses any more. How long is it since you have seen red meat? That's about all we get. I wish we would hurry up and get the fish trap fixed.

Once in a while I really do get a little homesick for you all. I used to think I never would, but you are awfully far away, and it is a funny feeling when you realize that there is nobody here who ever knew you before and no one I ever knew anything about, all really strangers from different backgrounds. People are living and partly living, half here and half that life before. It is pretty cockeyed sometimes, and I feel lost once in a while, but never sorry I came.

Of course, it is all different from what I had allowed myself to imagine. I think the most exciting thing was getting on the ship in San Francisco. Nothing has reached that peak since. Now it is personalities and trying to keep up with oneself. You can become narrow wherever you are and whatever you are doing, but that can't happen when one makes such a big break in life. Sometimes I feel as though I have always been doing this and that I know all these people very well. Then I am conscious of the temporariness of it all and I seem to be suspended in time.

This letter must sound as though I am homesick. I am not, just talking out loud, wondering about the whole situation. People are funny and all pretty much alike and I am no exception.

Much love,
Marcia

COFFEE and SYMPATHY
World War II Letters from the Southwest Pacific

[Yorkies Knob]
August 4, 1943

Dearest Family,

I really am doing more things that should appall a city girl, because I really am one in comparison to this life. I had to pick up 50 chickens today and haul a 44-gallon drum of petrol.

Both cooks are sick today, one with appendicitis and the other with gastritis. Arlene took them to the doctor, and Violet, the cook, will have to go into town tonight where she can be watched. She is reluctant to go, but the colonel is taking care of it. He is an awfully nice man and probably a good doctor. Everything happens to us and every day it is something different.

I went alone for the chickens with two crates because there were 50 of them. I found myself carrying out five chickens at a time by their feet. I had taken a shower and changed my uniform just before, which was a mistake because chickens are quite messy creatures.

It seems they are sending an ambulance out to take Violet in to the hospital tonight. While waiting for the ambulance we have been eating Italian bread, Gorgonzola cheese, and the colonel has a bottle of very good Scotch whiskey, something unheard of over here. We never drink in Red Cross clubs, but, because of the occasion, we are sitting down in the kitchen eating the cheese which came from an Italian man whom I found when I was looking for some thin spaghetti. Toni, the Italian grocer, also gave me some olive oil, a treasure as you know. We even have luscious big olives that a commander in the Navy brought us the other day — a big gallon jar of them. Honestly things like that are so exotic.

Arlene and the colonel have gone to get Violet ready for the ambulance, and I am waiting to direct the driver to the cottage. It is about 2:30 a.m., the latest I have stayed up since I have been in Australia.

Last night the dance was very crowded. I got four extra girls and with Elaine and me and a few of the officers' dates, there were enough partners for the stags. It is hard to get enough girls out here. There are always many more men than women and that means that we dance and dance and dance until we are good and tired. Everyone was happy and well fed.

I have been looking around the place to make improvements and I am gradually learning what has to be looked after to keep a place neat and running smoothly. As I say, the Filipinos work best when they see you working too. The Filipinos have usually been agreeable to me and do what I ask them. I told Juanito to clean the kitchen storeroom. He swept out the middle of it. I went in and cleaned all the shelves, put on new paper, emptied cases, got rid of rotten fruits and vegetables and Juanito washed down the place.

Marcia Ward Behr

Then we organized the canned goods. It took most of the day to put the cans in order. Things had just been tossed in any way, so you never knew what you had or how much of anything.

The china closet was next. Sonny helped me in there. He was willing to do most of the work. He did some cleaning, but I had to change the papers. Then I got Mr. Bradley, our Aussie neighbor, to hang the fire extinguishers, and today he went to work on the fish traps. With all the people who have worked on those traps, we ought to be eating fish by now.

It is pretty cold here. I am sitting in a breeze, so I think I shall stop and go wrap up in a blanket and wait until the ambulance comes. I'll write more Sunday.

Love,
Marcia

[Yorkies Knob]
Aug. 7, 1943

Dearest Family,

Yesterday the Red Cross Service Club and field workers ran a big football game. It took place in Cairns. Of course, it was pretty hot and that slowed up the game a bit, and then Army training is not quite the same as football-season training and the teams only practiced a couple of weeks. The score was tie, so everyone was happy.

Saturday night a new officers club was opened up with a dance. I stayed home because someone had to be here to entertain the few guests. I was sorry to miss it, but there are compensations. Today I had nothing better to do than clean up the yard. It was a mess and so I did it. Then I mended some Pianola rolls and was just going to take a shower, when a Syrian family, whom I met when I picked up some chickens last week, arrived on the scene. They are an amusing family. They live in Atherton, a village about 70 miles from here in the Tablelands. The father and mother are jolly, fat and rather sloppy-looking, and the daughters are young and beautiful.

The father owns a very nice hotel, probably the nicest for many miles around. They are presumably very prosperous, although you'd never know it from the way they dress and where they live. The house was clean but small. We had a delicious dinner there. The boy with whom I went used to visit them when he was stationed near their town. It was the daughter's birthday, and papa opened two bottles of champagne, so it was an exotic occasion.

Do not worry about my birthday. I have not heard from you recently — got a letter dated June 29 with clippings. Still waiting to hear wedding details.

                                        Love,
                                        Marcia

[Yorkies Knob]
August 12, 1943

Dearest Family,

I have just finished reading Sylvia's letter over again. It was certainly a good letter and I got a vivid picture of everything. Thank Tom for the toast. It certainly must have been a nice wedding, and how about the honeymoon? Did the car drive up in style and carry the lovebirds away to the wilds of the Adirondacks?

Last night we had a very successful dance but I was a wreck. The only way to make everyone happy at our dances is to get girls out here some way. Otherwise, just a few officers bring dates. Arlene and I get a terrific workout, and the officers with dates complain, because they do not even get a chance to dance with them.

Since I am not club director, and there is no one else here, I must be program director, so it is up to me to drag out girls. I have made a contact in the way of one of the leading social lights in town, a Mrs. Darley, and she has been very helpful. However, I can never be quite sure of the number of girls, if any, until the last moment. This week we were promised 20, so I arranged to have an Army truck bring them out here.

The poor girls arrived with a chaperon, all blown and dusty. They were late into dinner and everyone was seated, so I had to scatter them around and then sat down next to the chaperon. There were only twelve girls, some not too attractive and the others very cute. The chaperon kept an eagle eye on them. Six sat at a table by themselves. Most of the boys who dance came after dinner, so I had to gather the girls together and keep chatting until the dance started. I introduced them to a few boys and the chaperon could observe all.

When the music started, somehow or other, all the girls had partners and the chaperon sat on a bench in the dance hall. Next thing I knew a number of the girls were sitting with her on the bench minus partners. I remember dancing-school days and how no one likes to be forced to dance with anyone. The chaperon's daughter had a partner and I was thankful for that.

Arlene did not help me very much and, as I say, I did not want to urge anyone to ask the girls. However, later on they all seemed to have partners, but I must have had an anxious look on my face all evening. I succeeded in having a good time anyway and there were a lot of good dancers there. I met a boy who went to Harvard Law and was in a firm in New York. He knew a lot of Bennington girls and had been to dances there. He comes from Boston.

I knew the girls did not want to go back in a truck, so I finally got two officers who offered to take back some and I drove the rest. The chaperon wanted them all to go back together, so I explained that we would go in convoy and it would be quite safe. During intermission one pretty little girl was missing and that was an awful moment. When the music started again, she reappeared and we all breathed a sigh of relief.

Yesterday everything was in an uproar with the help. The Filipinos are getting pretty hard to handle, although if I ask them to do something and keep after them, they usually get it done, but you certainly have to follow up an issued order. No one wants to wash the dishes and I think the only thing to do is to switch jobs around, so that nobody has the same job all the time. Ricardo, who waits on table, wants to work upstairs because, when the work is done, he is through for the rest of the day and, to set up tables and clean after every meal, means he has to be on the job much longer.

Today I discovered that old Ramon had put the chickens in one little place, and the poor things were all on top of each other and getting no sun. Two of them had died and the yard was very messy. I let the little chicks out to run around with the big ones. It's better than to have them all cooped up and panting to spread out. The chicken yard needs another cleaning. More later.

Love,
Marcia

[Yorkies Knob]
August 17, 1943

Dearest Family,

I want to tell you everything and make it sound exciting, but there is nothing to say. The Filipino boys actually have us by the neck. They act as if they are too good for kitchen work. Mrs. Hayhoe, who is supposed to work upstairs only, had to wash the dishes today. And I dried them. There are so many things to see to and nobody really capable of doing it. I know I am not. I can do almost everything, but I don't feel like cleaning out the chicken yard and the grease traps, and those things have to be done or it is not healthy.

We have had two beautiful new refrigerators sitting in the outside alley for two months. With the new ones the cook could watch over the food more closely. We are now out of wood for the two kitchen stoves and I guess I'll have to go in the truck myself to get some tomorrow. The Filipinos are so independent. I have to ask them at least ten times to get something done.

The swamps had to be sprayed today and honestly I did not know whether I could get one of the Filipinos to do it or not, but I asked one of them and he agreed to do it. That was amazing, because it was afternoon and they all had quit working at noon. Butter is not to be wasted, as you know, yet they (Filipinos) cook up a mess for themselves of mashed potatoes and carrots and use a half-pound of butter and waste the rest. They say, "The Red Cross can get more," but we can't. We only get our ration. They break all the china when they get mad, and just laugh. We really should have two more girls and just keep the Filipinos to do the outside work, or simply lie around, which is what they like to do best. Mrs. Jeffrey, the cook, goes crazy with them in the kitchen preparing their own meals and snickering and making fun of everyone.

Last night the dance was very successful. I got seven extra, very pretty, local Cairns girls. I had to go into town to get them; an officer helped me out with another car.

A lot of boys brought dates and the orchestra was better than ever, so everyone was happy. Then too, it was a full moon and the nights are really beautiful here. It compares with any of the world's beauty spots. The moon somehow seems bigger and brighter, and it is a glamorous sight to see it glimmering through the palm trees over the ocean.

I received a nice letter from a Navy boy who was here for a while, and from two colonels and a letter from a young lieutenant in the Army. They all love this place and can't wait to come back. I do not blame them. It is beautiful and we have wonderful food, plenty of swimming and sunshine. I am not miserable, but I am disturbed. I refuse to wipe the dishes tonight. It is someone else's turn. That sounds familiar, doesn't it?

Lots of love,
Marcia

Marcia Ward Behr

[Yorkies Knob]
August 26, 1943

Dearest Family,

    Fancy Sylvia and Nan flying all over the place and I have never been up in a plane. I have been inside a Flying Fortress [four-engine bomber], though, and I shall get up before I get home, because train traveling in this country takes all the joy out of going anywhere.
    On Sunday Arlene let me go on a Navy picnic. We were going to a famous island. However, the sea was too rough so, we just went to a little beach cove. The Navy certainly had everything — American Coca-Colas, beer, ham, potato salad, pickles of all sorts, cheese, fruit and cakes. I did not bring my bathing suit, because it started out to be a cold day.
    I imagine if Tom's friend, Bob Areson, said he was in the North Pacific area, he must be near Alaska somewhere. I do not suppose he is anywhere near here, though he might be transferred someday. I still have not met anyone I knew before. I have not heard from Raine, who is now in the Army Air Corps. Maybe he is overseas or married.
    It is funny, you know, I sometimes do not feel as though I ever wanted to be an actress. That is the way. If you are not acting, you are not an actress. I wonder if I'd still be good. I wonder what is best in life, anyway. Take what comes, I say.
    This is a hard job over here, not in actual work, but it is a strain on your nerves. Some people are very nice, some are trying, and others a bore. Naturally, you like some people better than others, and being nice to everyone is sometimes painful. I am a very sincere person and honest with myself and others, so I shall not confuse the job with my own life.
    The fish trap does not work anymore and the shark net is still not in place. I am sure Arlene has tried. The iceboxes are still sitting there.
    I forgot to tell you about my birthday. When I returned from the picnic, I found we had six Air Corps boys staying with us. After dinner I had suddenly felt lonely and sorry for myself. No one had said, "Happy Birthday" to me. So I told Mrs. Hayhoe to say it to me, and made her promise not to tell anyone. Of course she did. Arlene had a case of beer. And so, after all the dinner guests had gone, Arlene, Elaine and our overnight guests sang "Happy Birthday" to me and we all went down on the beach and drank beer. It was fun, but I was very sleepy. The officers were all nice and hope to spend some of their leaves here. I am tired of writing and must go fix the flowers.

                                            Much love,
                                            Marcia

[Yorkies Knob]
August 31, 1943

Dearest Family,

Poor Tom! I suppose he is all over the horrible itch now. He should have known better than to fool around those red leaves in the Adirondacks. With poison ivy all over you, you just want to go into a coma for a while. I can certainly sympathize.

The new officers' club in town is open and it is a marvelous big floor under a huge circus tent. There is an orchestra of 12 pieces, probably the best in these parts. The tables are up on a platform all around the floor. I don't dance very long with any one person, which has advantages and disadvantages.

Tomorrow is Wednesday, dance night again here at Yorkies, and I must get some girls. The men (most of them) cannot drive civilians, so it is necessary to invite girls for the dances. There are so many things going on this week. There is a regiment dance on Thursday to which we have been formally, as well as personally, invited. I suppose most of the girls in town will be going to that. I do hope some will come to ours, and I hope the dance is better this week than last. Everyone seemed to have a good time but the hostesses. We thought it was awful.

Maybe I shall turn out to be luckier than Pat, especially if I could figure out some way to get to China from here. I shall do my best and, of course, take what comes. We are probably in the most coveted club in Australia. It certainly is beautiful, except for the rats — four-legged ones. I heard much noise last night and flashed my light. As I did so a big fat one crawled off the table and out the lattice work. I did not scream, but tucked in the mosquito net securely and soon went to sleep. They are annoying and they make so much noise! I am going to get the cat upstairs tonight.

Last week we killed a snake in the chicken yard, not poisonous but eight feet long. He had already eaten one little chick. As it gets hotter, more weird bugs and things appear. Oh dear, I shall just have to grit my teeth and live on. The mosquitoes are quite bad but, so far, no ill effects. Must go now to town for supplies.

Love,
Marcia

Marcia Ward Behr

[Yorkies Knob]
Sept 5, 1943

Dearest Family,

    Yesterday I received a long letter dated July 18 and a V-mail of August 25. However, I love the long ones. I also received a letter from Nan dated April 19. I thought something was funny when she thanked me for the Easter card. I was also pleased to get that little snapshot of Nan in slacks. Everyone says it looks just like me.
    The dance last Wednesday was very successful. The orchestra is large again and they set themselves up at one end of the hall. I got six pretty girls to come out and that always helps. So, with the dates the other boys brought, we seemed to have plenty of girls and not quite so many wolves as usual.
    We have been having quite a time here with our domesticities and Filipinos. Last Tuesday we discovered a case of 1000 cigarettes (which we keep for boys traveling through who cannot get their issues) was missing, also two hams. Gasoline has been stolen bit by bit and brooms and canned goods and anything you left downstairs, like my cards, would vanish. Every time I mislaid my fountain pen I would be positive it would never be seen again. Little things have been disappearing all along, but the hams, which are difficult to get, and the cigarettes were a little too much for us to stand. Naturally, we suspected the Filipinos because bottles of wine were found in the kitchen from time to time. Shoes left here by officers would appear later on one of the boys. One Filipino was actually seen fleeing with a new broom and a five-gallon can of petrol. He said he took the kerosene to clean his bike. Also the boys were seen riding around in a neighbor's truck. People do not waste their puny ration of petrol like that.
    Arlene turned it over to the police. The Filipinos have been annoying our Australian help in the kitchen with their profane language and actions. As a matter of fact, with few or no guests here some days, we did not feel so safe. Three girls alone at night and no locks anywhere. We are not always alone but once in a while. So we got protection from the army. Then Arlene told the commanding officer to get the Filipinos out of here as soon as possible. The day before they left they were out all night and did not come to work until ten and then they were hopelessly sluggish and sleepy. They did no work at all.
    That same day Arlene got the Army to promise to cart away the four young ones, leaving old Ramon, at seven that evening. It rained all day. A detail came to fix the new refrigerator and move out the old one. Also a detail to start on the

new bathroom for Arlene and me. Our other cook still had not come back from her appendicitis recuperation. We were short-handed but everyone was happy in the prospect of getting rid of the rascals.

The Filipinos were also deliriously ecstatic, because they thought they were at last going to war. Poor things. They have such a child-like psychology. They blamed Rita for the police suspecting them of stealing (by the way, the police really could not prove anything about the Filipinos) and punctured her bicycle tires in many places. Rita is a young, quick-tempered but bright, married girl who used to work in the kitchen, and now is waiting-on in the dining room where she is much happier. She was always screaming at the boys. So the Filipinos have gone and we now have old Ramon and Mr. Bradley, the engineer, two cooks, two waitresses and Mrs. Hayhoe who cleans upstairs. I think we shall get along wonderfully. As a matter of fact, everyone is so much happier. They do a lot more work, and I have a job finding something to do.

I went swimming today. By the way, an officer got a clipping from a U.S. paper whose columnist stated that (it was a write-up on "Somewhere in Australia") an afternoon at our rest home was his most enjoyable visit in all of the South Pacific. All right, what?

Love,
Marcia

Marcia Ward Behr

Eleanor Roosevelt Slept Here

Eleanor Roosevelt came to the South Pacific in September 1943, to visit the troops on behalf of her husband, the President, and report back to him her observations. By this time the Allies had secured New Zealand, Australia, Guadalcanal and bases in New Guinea. U.S. bombers flew continually from Guadalcanal to attack the Japanese-held islands in the Solomons that were blocking the Allied passage through the Bismarck Sea and beyond.

Mrs. Roosevelt and her party of high-ranking officers watched the Amphibious Engineers demonstrate landing barge exercises on the ocean at Yorkies Knob. Arlene and I were under very tight security for her visit to our club where the President's wife had dinner with us and spent the night.

There was divided opinion among the military brass about the value of a journey that required deploying planes and men to protect such an important person and transport her around the war zone. But, as Doris Kearns Goodwin wrote in her fine book *No Ordinary Time,* Mrs. Roosevelt's visit was truly a morale-booster for the fighting men. The generals and admirals realized at the end that her trip was a success.

Everywhere the President's wife went (according to Mrs. Goodwin's book), she told the troops that the President said "to tell you that you have done and are doing a wonderful job. He wants me to give you his deepest admiration and gratitude." And then she added some encouraging, loving words of her own. After hearing her one soldier remarked, "We liked this speech. Her sincerity permeated every word. I can tell you that after a year of listening to nothing but bassooning top sergeants and officers it was good to hear a kind lady saying nice things."

I wrote home about Mrs. Roosevelt's coming to Cairns, and a short article in the *New York Herald Tribune* mentioned me as being on the Red Cross staff at the Yorkies Knob Club.

COFFEE and SYMPATHY
World War II Letters from the Southwest Pacific

[Yorkies Knob]
Sept. 14, 1943

Dearest Family,

It seems ages since I last sat down to write to you, but when I explain you will understand that we have been busy.

I wish you could get a copy of the June issue of *REDBOOK* magazine. There is a marvelously intimate and colorful write-up of Mrs. Roosevelt. I must tell you that I read it after having been with her all one evening, sitting next to her too, listening to her. She is a wonderful woman and, if you can read that article, I think you can believe me that all Rose Franken [author of the play, *Claudia*] writes must be true. The First Lady spent the night with us at our club. She came in the late afternoon with her party of generals and admirals and "what nots" for dinner, the night and breakfast. You can imagine the preparation and previous secrecy of such an event. Touch me, please!

Everything began to happen at once, so naturally I thought something or someone unusual was coming, but I did not quite think it was the First Lady, though I knew she was in Australia. They began to scrape our road which had been four miles of sheer agony to drive over and we had not much hope of its ever being repaired. However, they did smooth it out. A detail came out to install those two refrigerators I have mentioned before, and they put in a septic tank and a bathroom for us. I remember thinking that was a little selfish, that the men should have a bathroom first. However, I soon discovered why all the work was being done. The whole visit was kept very secret, even from us up until the last moment. Elaine and I knew the day before and the help did not know who was coming until the very day of her arrival. Of course, the whole place was restricted and guarded. I felt very important bringing the marketing and having to pass through a number of sentinels before I could get home.

Mrs. R. arrived in the late afternoon. We were all dressed up in strict G. I. uniform — all insignia and pins. We wore our tropicals and Mrs. R. was in a heavier uniform. We had decided to change into our winter uniforms for dinner. Mrs. R. proceeded to change into a tropical one. However, it did not matter, but it was amusing. We had gotten gobs of flowers for the occasion and spent the night before arranging them all over the place. Everyone had been dusting and polishing for days so that everything would be just so. We put Mrs. R. out on the veranda where Arlene and I usually sleep. Then Arlene and I scrambled around in those windowless rooms off the upstairs porch. We borrowed a special bed for the occasion, which Arlene slept in the next night. She pulled her rank on me.

Mrs. R. is a strong personality. I think we all somehow knew what she would be like because no one was really jittery about her arrival. We did not worry whether she would like Yorkies Knob or not. We knew that she would be comfortable though things are not luxurious. If anything we understated her presence. When she came in the door and we all were waiting to greet her, I felt a little quivery for a moment, but after I had shaken hands with her (tell Sylvia she has a marvelous handshake, and really lovely hands) I knew everything would be all right.

Of course, the introductions were a little hectic for a moment and then getting the men to their rooms and seeing about the baggage. Since Yorkies had been taken over by the Army, naturally they could serve drinks if they desired. I immediately rushed around to see that the boys (two sailors had been lent to us to run errands and to wash dishes) had the ice and glasses and Cokes and all to go upstairs on the porch. I came into the kitchen and there was Mrs. R. with Arlene shaking hands with the help and looking over the kitchen. She was really charming and one soon feels a warmth from her that makes you want to smile back.

Mrs. R. rested before dinner and did not come down until it was served. We talked to the "brass" who were very charming. I had been nervous about spending an evening with such important people, but their friendliness soon dispelled any such qualms.

The dining room looked extremely pretty. One long table with little pitchers of delicate spring flowers placed all down the table. We had fruit juice, fillet of beef, peas, baked pumpkin, mashed potatoes and lemon meringue pie. The cook said Mrs.R. ate it all. I looked up once and saw the President's wife sitting there and it seemed unreal and yet natural. Think of coming to Australia to sit at the table with Mrs. Roosevelt. Throughout dinner she referred to "the President," later she spoke of "my husband" and at the end of the evening it was "Franklin."

The moon was getting full so the night was lovely and quite warm. Mrs. R. went upstairs for her knitting. When she came down, I went with her onto the porch and sat on the couch with her and talked for a bit. Not about anything in particular, but she said she was making socks for her sons and I soon discovered that she has observed a lot about the Red Cross in Australia. She also knows that the Washington Red Cross is a little bit in the dark about us over here. Later the others came out on the porch and we talked about many things. I asked her about public opinion on Russia in the States. I suspected optimism and pessimism, and I guess that is true. She told us about how cold it was in England, and her visit to the Queen Mother Mary. It was freezing in the royal dining room; after dinner the Queen Mother whispered discreetly, "Come to my sitting room where we can warm ourselves by my fire." Mrs. Roosevelt did not retire until eleven, and then she typed. She has unceasing energy. She is very relaxed, comfortable and kind. She has a wonderful sense of humor and we laughed a lot at her stories and she laughed at others. I know everyone was happy.

We had a good breakfast cooked on the grill outside. Mrs. R. said she would write to our mothers.

Love,
Marcia

[Yorkies Knob]
Sept. 15

Dearest Family,

I worked in the garden all morning and then went swimming and tried to get a little sunburn. I have a slight tan and a few freckles which come and go. Nevertheless, I look quite healthy, though I would not say I am much fatter, thank goodness. Today I ate a tremendous lunch: creamed chicken on toast, soup, tossed salad with tomatoes, lettuce and cucumbers, sliced fruit and your cupcakes with mocha frosting. It was a real ladies' luncheon. Some nurses were here for the day and they seemed to enjoy it too.

I had a shower after swimming and put on my new pink linen dress. It really looks very sweet and cool. It is nice to have something feminine to wear out here during the daytime. I cannot see that it matters if we are out of uniform. Everyone else is in shorts or a bathing suit. So what's the difference? You must have been surprised to see those clippings. Now you know, and after all the secrecy. It is so strange to have it come out in the New York paper. It is nice, though, she said quite a bit about the climate and so forth. I am certainly breaking into print. [Mrs. Roosevelt's "My Day" column]

I had a tough day shopping yesterday. I bought a whole bullock of beef that we can cut up ourselves. The butcher shop has no refrigeration. The butcher merely reaches for a carcass of beef hanging on a hook, throws it on one of the two cutting blocks, brushes away the flies and chops it in four big pieces. Tonight we shall have some of the meat braised, cooked in the oven with onions. Arlene never serves stew. I suppose that the men get it in the Army too much. However, good homemade stew might be liked. We can't throw away meat.

I thought I'd get off this letter to you because of my being so bad about writing last week. Your letters are always so nice, long and descriptive. They almost make me homesick, but I am strong-willed and can be happy somehow almost anywhere.

My love to all,
Marcia

Marcia Ward Behr

[Yorkies Knob]
Sept. 23, 1943

Dearest Mother,

Today I received two fat letters from you, one with Churchill's speech. Life goes on again here after all the to-do about Mrs. Roosevelt. It's usually quiet during the day and perks up at night. We know some awfully nice officers. They come and go, though. You ask if any one has brought out the funny side of me. Well, I do not know exactly. One boy who was here for a while made me funny. He was funny too, and we were always laughing. He was in the Navy. I heard from him once. I do not know where he is now. He came from New Jersey, so we used to talk about New York a lot. I really meet a great many people, never get to know any of them very well. Besides, they are mostly married and how horrible it would be it you ever fell for a married man!

I received a letter from Pete Owens today and I discovered that he is in the same squadron as a lieutenant who was here not long ago. It's a small world. I shall write Pete and tell him to look up some of those Air Corps boys who were here.

We have an excellent staff to do the work now. It is so much pleasanter with the Filipinos gone. We could use another man for the outside work, but somehow we manage quite well. I shopped today but it was terribly hot in town.

I suppose you hear of the good news on our war front. I remember how I used to read only about the European War and just occasionally would scan the Pacific headlines. Naturally, now it is quite the opposite and I often recognize and know people in the news.

We have heard nice reports from people about Mrs. Roosevelt's visit here. We have had thank-you notes. All in all, I think everyone enjoyed their little stay here. It seems like a dream now, except for the Army details working on new plumbing for the officers. So, now we shall be prepared for any visitor.

                                              Love,
                                              Marcia

COFFEE and SYMPATHY
World War II Letters from the Southwest Pacific

[Yorkies Knob]
Sept. 29, 1943

Dearest Family,

I received a letter from Nan today. Did I tell you I got a nice letter from Pete Owens? He knows where I am. I suppose he knows the A.P.O. number since he is around these parts. He has just been on furlough in a Red Cross rest area south of here, and said he had a wonderful time. I have heard that place is very nice — every sport available from tennis to riding.

Last night I had my first experience entertaining G.I.s. For the Wednesday dances we have had a very good 12-piece orchestra but they may not be here too much longer, so we decided to give them a little party here.

It is difficult to do much at our club because it is an officers' area. We have an outside dining room under the house as well as the one inside. So we planned to have the orchestra eat outside and Arlene and I would wait on them. Fortunately, I was able to get enough steak for them. As a matter of fact, I thought I had enough for everyone. I discovered later that the officers were given roast beef.

Arlene and I planned to dress in civilian clothes, so I pulled out my red silk dress which I have never worn overseas. We are not supposed to get out of uniform, you know, but we were in costume. As a matter of fact, it felt strange to be all dressed up like that and I felt embarrassed to come downstairs. There were a few officers here and, when Arlene and I came into the little lobby, they said that we never dress up like that for them and threatened to take off their bars and join the party. We said, "Nothing doing."

Arlene and I took the band out under the house near the grill and proceeded to cook the steaks. It was a comic sight to see us bending over the fire in all our finery. I was afraid our dresses would catch on fire, billowing in the breeze and the steaks flaring up into flames every time we dropped them on the grill. We cooked them all for 15 boys in about 10 minutes. Arlene and I waited on them and let Marge and Rita stay in the dining room with the officers.

After dinner the soldiers sat around and sang a bit of harmony while Arlene and I cleared the tables. Then we all went into the ballroom. Meanwhile one boy had sprained his ankle playing Ping-Pong. He jumped out a window after a ball and landed in a hole. That almost finished the party for the evening because he was in agony and had to be taken back to camp. One of the officers observed the predicament and offered the wounded soldier a ride back in his jeep. So we all traipsed back into the ballroom again.

Pretty soon the kitchen staff came all dressed up. Marge and Rita who are young and pretty, Mrs. Hayhoe who weighs 15 stone (210 lbs.) and is as funny as anything. She cleans upstairs. Mr. Hayhoe and their little four-year-old girl, Beverly, Mrs. Jeffery, the cook, who is like everyone's grandma. Violet, the other cook, did not feel well. Then there were Elaine, Arlene and I. We danced a bit and then Marge turned into a staff assistant and organized a game, "Musical Arms." It is like "Going to Jerusalem," only using people as props. Then we had to think of something else, so Marge said to play "Forfeits." It is like "Truth and Consequences." Each one hands in a trinket and someone acts as M.C. Mrs. Hayhoe took over. As each trinket is held over her head she decides what the person will do. It is a childish game but, with a mixed group of people, the young boys in the band, most of them quite shy and nice, and the rest of us, the things we had to do were very funny. Mrs. Hayhoe had a million things up her sleeve. Most of them were silly little kissing games, but they were really hysterical. We laughed and laughed. I had to go into a corner and sing and dance and cry and laugh. I did it with gusto. One of the boys asked me afterwards if I had done some acting, just from that little bit he thought I had.

All the boys in the band are excellent musicians and we have loved having them play. They are a big band and loud for our little dance floor but I like it. They stayed until twelve. We gave them cake and milk at intermission, just as we do for the officers, only cake instead of cookies. We had the food in the dining room, as we do at the dances. The boys seemed to have a good time. At any rate they were glad that this night they went home without having to pack up their instruments.

I forgot to say that we found a pretty good Victrola on the beach and we are using it, because our other one is broken. Our records are very corny: Johnny Doughboy Found a Rose in Ireland, Jersey Bounce and One Dozen Roses. I tried to get some more records from the local radio station. I borrowed 12 of about the same caliber as the above.

Wednesday night the dance was amazing. I brought out from town only five girls. The week before I could not get any. Had I known that the officers were going to bring so many dates this time, I would not have needed those girls. When we first started dancing there was not a single extra man. Arlene and I kept leaving the floor to make one stag. By ten o'clock the floor was simply jammed and there were only about five stags all night. I guess some of the officers were happy because they had a chance to dance with their dates. I only hope my girls had a good time.

We have been having perfect weather lately. Very warm in town. I can't wait to finish my shopping and get back home to Yorkies Knob again.

About my social life. Do not worry. I go out enough, and get away when I can. I was in a mood when I wrote that letter. I get enough laughs. I have not been to the officers' dance for about three weeks. However, I am going next week with someone who is fun. I stayed home on duty last Sat., but there were a lot of people here. I played Ping-Pong until I was blue in the face, then we sat around and talked. Someone brought me a case of Coca-Cola, an unheard-of luxury. We ended the evening by indulging in the luxury.

Yesterday I drove 50 miles to get some young ducks. We had chickens during the week, mostly ours but some from a farmer. I missed the dinner at Yorkies. I had mine with some Italians—good spaghetti. It was an awfully dirty place but the food looked clean and I wanted the ducks badly enough to eat anywhere. When I finally returned home, there was some spaghetti, salad and ice cream. I was a little weary shoveling strings into my mouth all day.

Elaine and I stayed home last night and entertained. We had heaps of fun playing doubles in Ping-Pong. We laughed and laughed. I like to stay at Yorkies when there are nice people here. Afterwards we sat around and wrote corny scripts, not really, but we jabbered along quite quickly and laughed some more. After that we had Cokes and Gorgonzola cheese.

Today is Monday, big shopping day. I woke up late, drank some orange juice and coffee, fixed up the laundry, collected checks for payments and finally got the shopping list and took off for town.

I had to call about a new orchestra and try to fix up the meat situation. Our meat has been awful lately; I think the butcher just gives us scraps. I decided it would be better to get 150 lbs. and keep it in the refrigerator. Then we can see what we have.

Thanks for the clipping about Mrs. R. I did make that remark to her but I had not been reading her column.

I must go and shop now. I just had lunch at the Red Cross Club in town. I am hoping for 12 girls for the dance this week, but they may back down at the last moment.

My love to all,
Marcia

[Yorkies Knob]
October 11, 1943

Dear Family,

I went to the dance Saturday night. It was my turn. I had not been for three weeks. I don't mind though because, when we don't go to the dance, people come here and see us. It is only fun to go with someone who is amusing anyway.

Else you might as well not go, especially now that only every fourth dance is cut-in. Arlene and I think we had better not go for a while because more and more people stay here Saturday night and we should be here to amuse them, if possible.

I have been very energetic the last couple of days. Saturday morning I got up at six-thirty to wake up two boys and get them some breakfast before leaving. They left at seven and, with Daylight Saving Time, it is only six. The sun was just coming up. Wearing a sweater it was just warm enough, so I took a stroll down the beach. I suppose I walked a couple of miles, anyway a mile and a half. Everything looks so pure and fresh at that time. I had forgotten. It's been so long since I have been awake to see a sunrise. I came back very hungry, but still breakfast was not ready. No others were up besides me and Ramon (the old Filipino lent by the army), who comes at six every morning to light the fire in the stove and make the coffee. Mrs. Jeffery, the cook, came and I asked her to make bran muffins. I wanted something good and different for breakfast. We have orange juice, cold or hot cereal and fried eggs and toast every morning. What more could you ask? Nevertheless, spoiled thing, I get tired of it. The bacon is not so hot here, at least I do not like it. It is never well cooked, always underdone. It is very lean and seems to have a strong flavor. Daddy is probably saying he would like it.

The next day, Sunday, I was up early to go to Green Island on the Great Barrier Reef, a celebrated sight here. The boat left Cairns at 8:30 a.m. This meant leaving Yorkies at eight. It was a wonderful boat ride and takes about an hour and a half. The water changes color all the way from gray to green, then blue, then deeper blue, then paler blue, then aqua, and then it gets clearer and clearer and clearer and paler and paler until you arrive at the island. There you can see right down to the bottom, though it may be more than ten feet.

It is just a little island but picturesque and tropical in every aspect. Small glass-bottom boats, not much larger than a rowboat, carry passengers to look at the fascinating underwater growth. Beautiful colors and small bright fish as you might see at Catalina. I liked it better, more primitive. The swimming was best of all. Just like a lake with clear, light blue still water. We wondered why we were the only ones in swimming. We found out why: the area is shark-infested.

We met some friends in another boat and they offered us Coca-Colas! What we had to eat was sad. We left in too much of a hurry to eat breakfast, just a cup of coffee and an orange. The officer who took me said we could get lunch over there. They did have a little restaurant but it did not offer much to hungry people. We had tea and small sandwiches when we arrived. We walked around the island in no time flat, changed into our suits, went for a swim, sun-bathed and then hurried back to see what there was for lunch. All the meat must have been mutton though under assumed names. I took the mutton. On the side were a few cold potatoes, some musty cold beets, plum pudding and hot tea to drink. Very Aussie but not filling.

Anyway, the day was perfect. We got home about 6:30, and I certainly ate my dinner. Afterwards we played doubles in Ping-Pong, very energetically and boisterously. Then I played singles until I thought I'd drop. Went to bed at eleven. I haven't done much today. Mrs. Roosevelt wrote to Arlene's mother and I am sure she will write to you. Got a nice letter from Aunt Lizzie.

                                          Love,
                                          Marcia

[Yorkies Knob]
October 17, 1943

Dearest Family,

Received Mother's V-mail about Pete Owens. How terrible! [He was killed in a plane crash.] I wonder if he got my letter. I have not written the lieutenant who wrote me, but I shall ask him. You know many of those announcements are false.

Last night we three girls had an unusual farewell party for Elaine White, our Australian secretary, who is leaving to go home to Melbourne. She has not been too happy lately and she has been here since the beginning, last November, and so it is best that she leaves. We shall miss her because she is a nice girl, quiet, sincere and intelligent. You have a picture of her in the snap of us three.

Unfortunately, she fell in love with a married Air Corps pilot who had stayed here. He loved her too but it was over. He was only married a short time before he left the States. I do not think that you can blame either of them but, after he left, Elaine almost fell to pieces. She is a little thing anyway. She has since gotten hold of herself pretty well.

You certainly have to be tough mentally to take this life. Can't let your heart be your guide. Naturally everyone gets romantic, especially the men, and one has to keep sensibilities working overtime.

Mrs. Roosevelt's visit was not enough for us. Once we had had a taste of fame and celebrities, we could not stop there. As a matter of fact, apparently, those in Mrs. R.'s party liked this place so much, they told Lady Gowrie (the wife of the Governor General of Australia — very much royalty) that she must stay here when she was in these parts. So she did. She came on a Saturday night for dinner with two Australian Army girl officers and spent the night. Of course, we had to move out again and go into our closet bedroom. Mrs. Hayhoe was cleaning in this room the other day and practically fell through to the floor below. Termites in the wood. Of course, my bed was right over the hole, but nothing happened. The floor held for one night. You can suffer any inconvenience for the privilege of having famous visitors.

Lady Gowrie was very sweet. However, I think we were all under a bit of a strain. I know Arlene was terribly tired. Other people were not restricted from the premises, as they had been for Mrs. Roosevelt. So we had a lot of people for dinner. We had some Australian and American brass and the mayor and his wife with her Ladyship.

The dinner was good — fruit juice, steak, fried eggplant in cracker crumbs, beans, potatoes, apple pie and cheese. People did not stay long, as Lady Gowrie was tired.

A group of us and one of her Army attendants went down on the beach. Someone had a bottle of Ron Rico Rum and the moon was just a mite beyond full. We spilled most of the rum, but nobody cared anyway. Arlene did not come down. She had a splitting headache and went to bed. I had to turn out the lights which I did at midnight and then I had to go meet the 2 a.m. train from the south, supposedly bearing our new secretary to take Elaine's place.

To go back and pick up the disjointed thread which is the theme of my letter. Remember I mentioned the farewell party? Elaine has been waiting to go for nearly a month. However, she could not leave until her successor arrived. She was to show her the accounting routine, files etc.

Elaine came here "green," had never been a secretary and could just barely type. She used to do progressive kindergarten work. Through her intelligence and mistakes she learned the work, and has been wonderful in her job. She has not left a thing undone and has fixed everything, so nothing really needs to be done for almost a month. This would give the new girl time to catch on to the work.

One of the girl-lieutenants with Lady G. asked Elaine how long she had been here and she mentioned that she was going home. So, they asked her to ride in their plane leaving in a couple of days. We expected the new girl to come on that train — which would give Elaine almost two days to show her the system. A captain and I met the train, waited around the station until nearly 3 a.m., both of us exhausted, and no girl. The next train would not arrive until after Elaine had gone.

Arlene has many faults as have we all. I am beginning to find a number of good points about her that outweigh the bad ones. I decided that she could not make me disagreeable and dislike her, but that we would like each other. She has a bad disposition sometimes and says mean things without thinking before she speaks. Since the Filipinos have gone, the household has been running quite smoothly. I know I have been happier and Arlene has been a lot sweeter. She is an attractive girl, bright with a quick sense of humor. She expresses herself very easily and well with a short story or newspaper imagination technique — if you get what I mean. The other day she said she met someone she thought she could marry. She is not passionately in love with him, but he must bring out the best in her. I have noticed that she has mellowed since she has known this person — just a short while.

Arlene was white and tense when she realized that Elaine had made up her mind to leave by plane anyway, in spite of the fact that the new girl had not arrived. She was so mad because she had absolutely no control over the situation, so mad that she snapped at everybody. She did not snap at me but came to me for understanding. She felt that Elaine had gotten everything out of the Red Cross and had given it very little, considering, and now was not staying to finish the job. I do not know how complicated the system is, but I imagine it will inconvenience Arlene some. However, she has signed everything and Elaine has worked in advance and the clerk in town is supposed to help, so her leaving cannot be so tragic.

Still, Arlene looked only on her side of the situation, feeling that Elaine was leaving her in a lurch. She was blind to Elaine's feelings. I knew that I would have let her go without any fuss and worried away at the thing myself. Arlene would come to me and say how Elaine had gotten this and that and the other from her job and, when she no longer felt happy here, she was selfish in grabbing at the opportunity to fly. Then Arlene wrote a letter to headquarters not recommending Elaine. She showed it to me and I blame myself for letting Arlene send that letter without an argument. On the other hand, it may be just as well because, as things soon developed, Arlene's conscience may make her retract her statements.

The other day one of our good friends, especially Arlene's, had given us a bottle of Sparkling Hock (Champagne) and told us it was for Elaine's farewell party. Just before dinner, when Elaine was packing, Arlene asked me to ask her when would she like to open the bubbling bottle.

I went in to Elaine. She looked tired, probably because she had been working on the books. To the question she said, "before dinner." I went down to get the bottle from the ice chest and the glasses. (Please do not think we drink all the time. As a matter of fact, we hardly ever drink but I have to mention the drinking in this letter because it is part of the plot.)

When I came back I stopped in Elaine's room. Oh, before that I had asked Elaine to give me back the Red Cross pin I had let her wear. Arlene told me to get it back. I suppose that was the final blow to poor little Elaine. I came into the room and she looked at me and said, "I can't go in there and drink to my farewell with Arlene, knowing that she feels the way she does about my going. I just cannot do it." Then she sobbed. I put my arms around her and said, "Never mind, just forget it, pretend nothing has happened and everything is all right, just try to think you are going with her best wishes." (The other day I heard Arlene say to Elaine, "You are not going with my best wishes.") Then I mumbled, feeling very guilty, "I will write to the Red Cross." I was thinking about Arlene's letter.

I must say I rather revel in these dramatics. I somehow cannot think they are real. I suppose that is my Stanislavski training. I feel as though I am doing a good piece of acting, very professional and, at the same time, I am conscious all the time that what is going on is not real and very soon again the mood will change. I felt very satisfied with this moment of suffering. I do not think I was conscious of this at the time but, looking back on it now, I see that I almost enjoyed the drama. Am I hard boiled? No, because I was crying, too, or at least getting ready.

I came back into Arlene and she was stewing over a piece of paper. I did not say anything. She called Elaine, apparently to ask her something about the paper. She went to Elaine's room. I followed and stood in the doorway. Elaine was in the middle of the room. She said, "I am sorry, Arlene, but I cannot go in there and drink a farewell toast knowing the way you feel. I know you are right, but I just say, I do not think you are very kind. Everyone else is glad I have this opportunity and anyone else would not mind the little inconvenience of going over the books with the new girl. Sometimes I have not been very happy here, but I have done the best I know how, and I have worked way ahead. You are the club director and have signed everything. You can show the girl. She could not know less than I did. I did not know the difference between an invoice and a bill of sale. I am sorry but I do not feel that I am letting down the Red Cross by going."

Elaine was speaking very simply and looking right at Arlene. If she had stopped talking or looked away, she would have cried her heart out. I was staring at Elaine and glancing at Arlene. Tears were running down my face as I watched and waited. I just knew everything would be all right, but I did not know how many moments it would take. Arlene spoke in a low controlled voice.

"You have gotten a lot out of the Red Cross. I have been satisfied with your work, but I am looking out for my club. I am not thinking of myself. I have a lot of things on my mind." She went on in that vein. It sounded lame to me but she stood her ground and Elaine helped her.

"I cannot think I am doing the wrong thing by the Red Cross," responded Elaine. "Don't lose your temper, Elaine." "I am not losing my temper. I am crying. That is why my voice went up. I still say," Elaine went on, "You are right, but you are not very kind."

Arlene said, "Yes, I am tough and hard-boiled." This in a sarcastic tone, then she said, "I have had to fight my way always." Elaine was really crying. I was crying. I said something about forgetting the whole thing. Nothing very brilliant.

COFFEE and SYMPATHY
World War II Letters from the Southwest Pacific

I think Elaine cried quietly a moment and I was watching Arlene. Her expression softened. She slowly went to Elaine and gently put her arms around her and said, "I do not want you to go away like that, either."

I ran out of the room sobbing. I grabbed a bath towel on the way, flung myself on my bed and cried into the towel and pillow. I think I was about ready for a crying spell, anyway, so I indulged. While I lay there, Elaine and Arlene overcame their strained relationship. Soon Elaine came out and I said. "Now we can have a bang-up farewell party. I just knew everything would be all right because you are you." It was just a matter of time, one or two minutes. The emotion had to run its course. (Now I appreciate the time it takes to fill a dramatic moment.) Elaine was laughing and I laughed and smiled. We looked in the mirror. We looked awful. I had cramps anyway. My hair was hanging. (By the way, my hair is all right — quite pretty usually. Syl asked about that. So far so good. It is quite golden from the sun.)

I went into Elaine's room to get Arlene. She was standing with her back to me holding onto the bed. She said, "In just a moment." She might have been thinking about the letter, I don't know, but she must have been doing a lot of thinking. I believe she was marvelous to break down. It means a lot more when someone like that...

Oct. 20. Tremendous break here. A car drove up. It was Arlene. She had taken Elaine leaving very early yesterday morning to catch a plane from another town quite far from here. I ran out to meet her and who should step out but Elaine! Fate works in strange ways. The plane had engine trouble and Elaine could not fit on the other plane that they sent up for Lady Gowrie. All that fuss just fizzled into nothing.

I took Elaine into town yesterday afternoon to see what could be done about getting another plane and maybe catch Lady G's plane further down. It finally turns out that she cannot catch the special plane, but will probably get something out of here in a day or so.

This is a long letter, I know. We have all been tired. It has accumulated since the dance last Wednesday. We stayed up late and talked with four of the nicest Navy men who have ever stayed here. Their ship docked in Cairns to take on supplies before heading for New Guinea. I think they were all married but one lieutenant, named Jim Wilder, who was very attractive and said he was separated from his wife. The dance was fun and afterwards I went swimming with them. The next night I took the kitchen staff to the movies and, when I got back, Lt. Wilder and the other men were here again. I did not go swimming but stayed up until nearly two when they left. The next night I managed to go to bed about 11 p.m. Saturday I did not go to bed until 3:30 a.m. because I met the train which was supposed to have the new secretary and did not. Sunday night we sat up until one o'clock talking to some old friends who were leaving the area. Monday night we went through the emotional farewell party orgy. Last night we went to bed pretty early but I am still tired.

>
> Love,
> Marcia

[Yorkies Knob]
Oct. 27, 1943

Dearest Family,

By the way, how is the gas situation? It seems to be better. You seem to be eating well enough, though I suppose it takes a lot of figuring out to make different meals from a much smaller selection.

Hot weather and dryness here make fewer vegetables for us and it is hard to plan meals. We are eating very well, though. I suppose better than any other country in the world.

Sometimes I get a little restless. I wonder if I am really doing enough. However, when boys come back who have been away and I see how much they appreciate this place, I suppose it is valuable work. I can't think of any place I would rather be in Australia. I shall just wait and see and, if I am a good little girl, something good will happen to me. That's right, isn't it?

I feel myself getting disagreeable, especially when I notice Arlene is getting that way. I suppose she does have a lot to worry about. It is hard to get labor. We are always needing wood for the kitchen stoves and the engine for the lights is not behaving well. Mrs. Jeffery, one of the cooks, went to the hospital last week. Kidney trouble. She is really too old for a steady job like this, so Arlene should look for another cook. They are practically impossible to find. The other one got a letter saying her husband is wounded. She is restless and having her little girl here while she is working gets on her nerves. Mrs. Hayhoe, the upstairs woman, is supposed to have a rather indelicate and painful operation, so we are in a bit of a fix.

Last night we had one cook and one waitress (the other one took her day off) and 50 people for dinner. I had helped upstairs in the morning, went to town for meat in the afternoon, came back and had a swim, went for our laundry, had a shower, got dressed, helped set the tables, waited on table, ate in between and then helped wipe the dishes.

After all was over, I came in and sat on the porch with the guests. We made lemonade and about midnight I turned off the lights. Do not misunderstand me, I would rather be busy like that any day than sit around. Nevertheless, we could use a little more manpower out here.

Did you receive the coconut I sent? Arlene's mother received hers.

You asked me once if anyone ever brought out the funny side of me. The other night the lights did not go on at all. Arlene suggested we have a fire on the beach. There were about twelve officers who stuck around after dinner. We all collected wood and went down on the beach with blankets, Victrola and chairs. Something got into me. One officer was there and he is very funny. Somehow we started calling each other "Rosebud" and "Stinker." We were a vaudeville team and that night we were just crazy. Everyone was listening to us and laughing. We jitterbugged in true style. He threw me all around. I danced on his feet like a rag doll in a marathon dance. We polkaed and gavotted and, to anything they played, we made up a routine. We really laughed that night.

We made a big pitcher of lemonade and threw apples on the fire. We just left them there to turn into apple sauce. We finally left about midnight when the last ember was dying out. Times like that are fun. I am sure no one is conscious of a lack of spontaneous amusement but sometimes I realize it would be better if it happened more often. I hear the lunch bell now. We have a detail working on the shark net. Arlene has really put her all into getting that up. She started working on it last February and at last we are getting some cooperation

Do not mind me and my changing attitudes. I just tell you what I am thinking at the time. I may change next week.

Much love to all,
Marcia

[Yorkies Knob]
Nov. 5, 1943

Dearest Family,

I have really been getting mail from you in the past few days. I did not realize my letter about Mrs. Roosevelt was anything. I must have written a lot.

Not so much has been happening lately except that we seem to be losing our staff, one by one. I told you one cook went to the hospital. She has kidney trouble and is over sixty. They are really old in this climate at that age and she may not be able to come back, at least not full-time. Marge, one waitress, left yesterday.

Rita, the other one, is leaving, maybe for good, because her husband is home on leave. Violet, the other cook, is agitating to go and just hanging on until we find a new cook. Mrs. Hayhoe wants to get her house back from the army and stop working. Luckily, we do not have many overnight guests now. We have quite a few for dinner always and for both meals on Sunday.

You would have laughed to have seen me on horseback the other day. A friend of mine, who has since left, wanted me to go on a picnic. We had been planning one for some time, but, somehow or other, every time we fixed a date, something would keep me from going. I did the marketing in town early and we left for the picnic a little after noon. We had been told about a place that was about 45 miles away. It is quite a pretty drive there and the road is quite good even in a jeep.

I made ham and Gorgonzola cheese and tomato and tuna fish sandwiches, took also some fruit and two Milky Ways that were presented to us by a Navy boy. They were quite a luxury. I succeeded in getting a small thermos bottle and Rex had one too. I put milk in mine. He didn't have anything in his. We started eating the sandwiches before we were halfway there. Rex is funny as anything and Arlene says we are good stooges for each other. He makes me funny, though, and we do laugh a lot. I would get tired of too much of him because sometimes I do not feel funny and he goes right on.

We finally came to another town beyond our town, where there is another Red Cross club. Here we decided to fill the other thermos with milk. Also we ate a big chocolate sundae. We were full now and had only gone halfway to the falls where we had expected to spread out our picnic. Rex kept mentioning horseback riding and for me to be on the lookout for some horses to hire. I said something about not having ridden for years and then not much. I think the only time I did was on that old truck horse in the Rockies when we had to walk them most of the way. However, I rather liked the idea of riding and I was not at all afraid, only nervous that I would look as though I had never ridden before.

I only had on an old denim skirt with shorts underneath, so my legs were bare. Finally, as we turned off on an old dirt road to the falls, we saw a pretty young girl on horseback and asked where we could find some horses. She directed us and we had a little trouble persuading a Mr. Dowling, a cane farmer, to let us ride. We had to go out to the fields to catch them. I took the smaller one. I hopped up on him like a veteran and then didn't know how to make him move. Rex's horse started first and then mine followed, but not very quickly. The farmer gave me a stick. He said, "Then he will know who is boss." And off we trotted. The straps of the stirrups chafed my legs and I think I would have preferred going bareback. I gave the horse a bit of a switch and that was all he needed. He started to gallop. One of my legs came out of the stirrup. I tried to go up and down with the horse and did pretty well. The horse did not go too fast anyway. We had to walk them down a slope to the falls and we tied up the horses halfway.

It was a pretty place — huge boulders and beautiful clear water splashing all through, with clear little pools of water nestling in and around the rocks. There were many levels and I suppose the falls were quite high and during the rainy season plenty of water must pound down. Not a soul was anywhere around. We climbed down and found a tremendous flat boulder and stretched out on its smooth surface that seemed almost soft in the warm sun. Rex went to sleep and I hung my toes in the deliciously cold, clear water.

Of course, we left our picnic and thermoses back at the farm. After a half hour we started back. I suppose we had come a couple of miles. Now comes the ride back. You know horses on the home stretch? I had forgotten. At any rate the horse started at a fast gallop. Mine was way ahead of Rex's. I tried to stop my horse a couple of times and gave up. My feet were both out of the stirrups and I had a fierce grip on the harness. I kept laughing all the time, so that I was fairly relaxed. I knew there was a fence soon and the horse would have to stop. I was still on him when he did. My, it was fun. I loved it.

However, that is not all. When we got back to the corral, I started to put the horse before the stall, because the farmer had said to tie them up in a stall when we finished. I put the horse in position in front of one and was about to get off. The roof of the building sloped down just high enough for the animal to go in with perhaps six inches to spare. Rex said, "Get off the horse before you go in." But the horse made a dive for the stall and I, in the nick of time, bent over backwards and lay flat along its back and just saved myself from being cut in half. I did not feel as though it were a narrow escape, but Rex was quite ashen.

I was a little stiff for a couple of days from my experience, but I am willing to go again. It is certainly fun, only I should learn a few things to say to a horse and I need to wear long pants.

Arlene is going to mail this letter in town and I have to go swimming with a guest. I do not want to go. It is too early in the morning and I want to rake the garden, but what can you do?

                                            Love,
                                            Marcia

Marcia Ward Behr

[Yorkies Knob]
Nov. 10, 1943

Dearest Family,

    In the mail today I received three Sunday Times and the Garden City News. Apparently the News has been running the letters of some Red Cross girl in Ireland. I thought them a little dull but then maybe my letters are just as dull with all our domestic problems. The letters did say that no night was warm enough to go without a fire. I would perish with the cold. So far I seem to thrive on the heat. And so far we always have a delightful ocean breeze. I have used a blanket almost every night, but it is still spring and summer will come.

    Joy of joys, I went up in a plane the other day. It was most unexpected and I know every other ride will seem tame after this. Not having had any experience with which to compare my first ride, I was not quite sure whether it was wild or not. We gave our Yorkies Knob plenty of "buzzes" that seemed daring to me. We went way up high and I was freezing — then fast down again where the air was very warm — always traveling at 300 miles per hour. In fact, it seemed a bit slow to me.

    The pilot (just two of us — I was alone in back and he in front) strapped me in, draped a Mae West and a parachute around me, put earphones on me, stuck a thing in my neck to get vocal vibrations for telephoning, and off we went. Just as we started on the take-off, I remembered I had forgotten to ask how you opened the chute. Oh well, I thought, I can ask him over the phone. The pilot had just finished fixing the plane in the morning and this was a test flight. When he asked me, I hesitated for a moment. He looked so young and how did I know, maybe he had only been flying a short while. He said he had been over here eight months. Well, he had to know something in that length of time. The chance was too good and comes too seldom, at least for such a good ride with a fighter pilot.

    The take-off was fast and perfect. I was up in the air and everything was just as I expected only we did not seem to be going very fast. I remembered about the chute. I heard the pilot say something to me. I guess he said, "Are you all right?" So I said, "Yes!" Then I started to ask about the parachute. He did not get a word I said. I gave up and said, "Go faster." I do not know whether he understood or not but we went faster. We buzzed the knob a lot and I could see the people clearly down below. My windows were open and I dropped a piece of Kleenex to them. We went miles down the coast and over the country. It was perfect. We got way up above the clouds and seemed to be higher than the mountains. I think the difference in temperature made me cold and a little icky, but I would not have admitted it for the world.

We stayed up for an hour and a half. What a ride! Arlene was certainly happy to see me back again. Apparently we were flying below the treetops when we buzzed the club. So, I say a transport plane would seem a bit dull after that.

The domestic situation isn't much better. Arlene is going to see a prospective cook tomorrow. Rita's (one of the waitresses) father was killed by a railroad train the other day. Her mother was going to help us out but she won't come now, I suppose.

I found a couple of Christmas decorations today. We shall have to start planning for that day. It will be awful to be away from you all but we shall make the best of it.

Love,
Marcia

[Yorkies Knob]
November 15

Dearest Family,

Onward to Christmas, but it certainly doesn't feel like it. I am sorry I am not sending you more from this side, but there is not much here. I am glad the coconut arrived. I just sent it as a joke.

Arlene called from town today and said my letter to Pete Owens had been returned so I guess that is an answer. What a shame. This war is awful. I still feel far away from it. In fact quite marooned. I know a lot of boys up there now, but they seem pretty far away and I may never bump into them again. I write to some. I guess letters mean everything. I said to one boy who had been there a long time that I supposed he thought of food above all else and he said, "No, mail comes first."

Some Red Cross girls are in New Guinea. As you can read in the papers, it is pretty safe there now. I wonder if I would like to go there. Malaria is a danger but it is prevalent here too. However, so many people say it is miserable up there, and others say they would rather be there than here. Nevertheless, I am getting a bit restless. I think I have been here too long. I have decided to take my leave right after Christmas.

Right now this place seems to be just a restaurant. We are terribly short-staffed. Last night I helped to prepare the dinner and then I waited on table. I do not mind too much, but I do mind when strangers think I am a waitress and yell, "Hey, Miss!" or "Hey, Waitress!"

There are a few nice Navy officers who have been coming here quite often. Once, on a Saturday night, they said they did not like it because I always went with Army officers. So, they asked if I were going to be home the next Saturday and they would come out and bring a picnic. Arlene and Marie Samers, the new secretary, went to the dance and I stayed home with the Navy, so to speak. We had a good time sitting on the beach and eating hot dogs until the end of the fire.

During the week I received a little note from one of them saying they would like to repeat the performance. Arlene stayed home and Marie went to the dance. We just sat around the fire on the beach under the most beautiful tropical moon. We talked, laughed and sang. One by one people left until there were just three of us and we night owls stayed up far into the night. Finally, I went because I was cold but the two boys stayed up until dawn. I was the only one around for breakfast the next day. I rang and rang the bell but nothing happened until nearly eleven. By that time the stove was being used for lunch, so they had to have boiled eggs and bread instead of toast. I got it for them. Everyone looked a little dark around the eyes but they seemed cheery.

The dances in town are not so much fun any more so I think a picnic was a good alternative. Of course, the Navy supplied everything, and I really felt more like a guest than the usual hostess. Friday night I did go to an officers' club dance, quite small but I enjoyed myself. Tomorrow I am going there for lunch. They have lunch at 11:30, just a little later than our breakfast but I'll only eat one egg instead of two.

I have not gained any weight, surprisingly enough. Some days I have a big appetite and some days I do not eat at all, so I guess that cancels any pounds I may put on during my gorging period. I ate lots of ice cream yesterday. We had a surplus. I made ice-coffee with ice cream, had pineapple and chocolate fudge sundaes and oh, just had a wonderful time. Whenever I'd get bored I would just run out to the kitchen and eat ice cream. You should have been here, Mother.

Love,
Marcia

COFFEE and SYMPATHY
World War II Letters from the Southwest Pacific

[Yorkies Knob]
November 21, 1943

Dearest Family,

I am so hot I could jump right in the water! However, I must write to you. We just finished serving at least a hundred people. We are short-staffed now, so we were in for a beating. I have been doing all the menus lately.

The other day Arlene had arranged the menu and she had ordered canned beans. I found some fresh ones in town, really young, and in this climate, if you do not use them right away, they get soggy and mildewed in no time. When I got home, I suggested we have them for dinner. Arlene said, "No, we can't get them done in time." I started on them anyway and the cook helped me. Arlene was furious. I laughed and said she could fire me. The dinner was a pale, boarding house affair and needed the fresh beans. Well, we had them. Arlene talked to me as "boss" and employee. "I appreciate your helping in the kitchen, but I do not want my orders changed, is that clear?" Oh well, I do not care. We get along all right. I suppose it was wrong of me to force the beans.

Last night we had some fun. A lieutenant, who had done some directing for a summer theater, got hold of us and two officers and we played "The Game." Then he introduced an activity that consists mostly of hitting people over the head with a newspaper when they do not say the right thing. We laughed and laughed. Finally we had quite an audience who joined in and everyone had a good time.

Afterwards we ate ham sandwiches and milk and some large Schrafft peppermint patties compliments of the Navy. Then we went swimming, then I played Ping-Pong until I was so hot I could have gone swimming again.

It is summer now, but there is usually an ocean breeze. I certainly love all your letters and I know the family all reads mine.

                                            Love,
                                            Marcia

[Yorkies Knob]
late November

Dearest Family,

It is funny how sometimes it is a joy to write a letter but, for the past couple of weeks, I must force myself. I suppose it is just another phase and it will pass.

Marie Summers, the new Aussie secretary, just asked me if Sylvia would buy some perfume and send it — Shalimar's Christmas Night or Tarragon by Coty, also, some dark red nail polish. Use my money.

We are becoming a restaurant, not a rest area. Thanksgiving dinner was perfect. We had turkey and cranberry sauce, pumpkin pie and ice cream. There were two sittings and everyone loved it.

Arlene has gone away for two days. I do not want to go away for two days. I want to go away.

The trouble with me is, I think, I need new territory to conquer. I have been here long enough. They usually transfer people around if they have been in a place six months and I have been here nearly seven. I am tired or maybe I have not been concentrating on the right thoughts. I need someone to talk to, I presume, and all the ones I know seem to have gone. It is lonely out here at times and yet one could hardly call one's time one's own. Tonight there were 108 people for dinner and we have only one waitress, so all of us pitched in and everyone was jolly and laughing. Oh, it was hot, though. We had nine tables of six in each sitting. After the first we carry out all the dishes, then they are washed — fresh doilies are put on and the tables all set up again. That means all the bread, milk, butter, jam, cream and sugar has to be replenished. It is a job. The first sitting is at 6:30 and we try to have the next one at 7:30. We rang the gong for number two at 8:15. Not too bad. I was wringing wet at the end of the business. I have just come from helping to clear up the final dishes.

I must not let things get me, but I constantly see what needs doing. We have no one to tend the garden, the lister bag for drinking water must be changed oftener and cleaned out. The icebox is sometimes on "on the nose", as Mrs. Hayhoe says, and you have to prod Ramon to clean it. Odd odors pop up, sometimes it is the grease traps or the sinks. Flies gather and the garbage needs burning. Added to all that there is my personal laundry to do. We have no one to do it. Mrs. Hayhoe does Arlene's for her, because she says she is not capable. I ironed some of Arlene's things yesterday to save Mrs. Hayhoe.

I do not know what would happen to this place without that "gem" Mrs. Hayhoe. She was so understanding when she came upstairs one day and found me dissolved in tears. She finally made me laugh by swinging her large hips in a "hula hula" and I collected myself again.

I suppose I shall get a letter from you tomorrow. That would help. I can imagine how much mail means to the boys up north who have nothing, not even a bed or any material comforts. I should look around me and count my blessings. However, one has these sad, sad moments and, then, ecstasy is so much more wonderful in contrast.

Happy birthday to Nan. I shall send her a cable.

Love to you all. I am really happy in my work and something will happen soon to add to my happiness, I am confident.

Love,
Marcia

[somewhere in New Guinea]
November 29, 1943

Dear Marcia,

Sorry I took so long in sending you your copy of this snapshot. The other copy has gone to New Orleans to my wife to show her how lucky we were in Australia in having such cute American girls to look at and dance with.

I was unable to get my roll of films developed before I left Australia.

I often think of good old Yorkies Knob. If I ever get back for a visit, I am going to make a better attempt to make a better impression on certain people.

I think all the officers in the 2nd ESB will always have a fond memory of your well-run place. All of us had many happy moments there. If I don't see you again, be sure to visit New Orleans someday when you get tired of New York. You would enjoy it, I promise.

Good luck!
Major John Paul Tobin

[Yorkies Knob]
Dec. 1, 1943

Dearest Family,

I am terribly tired tonight. It was Audrey's (the waitress, the only one) day off today. Last night Arlene said I could sleep this morning but I never have hopes of that. At 8 a.m. she realized that there was no waitress so, naturally, Marie and I came down to help.

I was slightly annoyed at breakfast, as I think I am capable of deciding what to do and when. We were all three waiting on table, including good, kind Mrs. Hayhoe, and there were only about ten guests. You have to stand and wait for the eggs anyway, so one person could easily have done the whole business. One of the officers had been trying to persuade me to sit down, but I knew there was orange juice to squeeze and coffee to pour before I could have my breakfast.

I finished squeezing and pouring and I sat down but, realizing I must wait on myself, I jumped up and went for coffee. Arlene stopped me and in her most autocratic manner, she said not to sit down yet. So I put the coffee down at my place and went back in the kitchen to join Marie and Mrs. Hayhoe waiting for individual plates of eggs. When I returned to the dining room I saw that Arlene was sitting in the very seat I had left and was putting sugar in my coffee. She said, ("amusingly"), "I am fixing your coffee. I said ("amusingly"), "I don't take sugar, thank you," and went out into the kitchen. I finished waiting on the few people. Marie and Mrs. Hayhoe had decided they were not needed, and then I ate my breakfast in peace in the kitchen.

After breakfast I watered the garden and pulled up all the weeds. Then I helped a bit in the kitchen, and swept out the dining room, the lobby and the porch. I straightened up my room and then it was lunch. We had only two guests, so that was easy. After lunch I fixed all the string beans for supper. I raked up all the butts and papers around the ballroom. It is always a mess after the Wednesday-night dances. Then I came upstairs and washed out a lot of my clothes. Arlene insisted upon my resting at 4:30, which was nice of her. I do not have to do this work, but it would never be done and it embarrasses me to see the filth. Besides, Violet, the cook, works twelve hours a day and she is not happy about that. Arlene set up all the tables for supper. Marie helped serve in the kitchen and I waited on table with Mrs. Hayhoe.

I talked to a very nice officer, Nelson Page, a New York architect. I am sure I have met him before somewhere. We discussed New York and the theatre pretty thoroughly. He was very intelligent about the latter. His wife's name was Auchincloss. He spoke about the Blue Hill Troupe, the Gilbert and Sullivan singers, but I do not remember where I have seem him before.

This is a lovely place but I am a bit weary of it. They usually transfer people after the length of time I have been here.

The shark net is practically down. It lasted about a month. Gee, I am tired. An Aussie major just came to see me. Oh, dear!. Merry Christmas.

Love,
Marcia

COFFEE and SYMPATHY
World War II Letters from the Southwest Pacific

[Yorkies Knob]
Dec. 6, 1943

Dearest Family,

    I certainly keep busy washing and ironing in this climate. The other day it was about the hottest I have ever felt anywhere. Just sitting still I was completely soaked. It was not so bad today, a good breeze.
    I spent a couple of hours on the beach today and look a lot better. I think my unhappy period is over for a while. At least I have tipped over something inside me that was too brimful and I am much relieved. It makes me look better and, with a healthy sunglow, a few freckles and shiny hair, I feel better.
    I am enclosing a letter and a picture taken the same day as those others I sent you. The picture was taken by Major Tobin and he is not the man in the picture.
    I have been getting the *New York Times* pretty regularly. I do hope, Mother, you are not working too hard. Cannot you possibly get a cleaning woman to help you? Use my money. Did I tell you that the watch arrived? Thank you very much. Saturday night I went to the officers' dance, thought I would try it again. I had a marvelous time, much to my surprise.

                                           Love,
                                           Marcia

[Yorkies Knob]
December 13, 1943

Dearest Family,

    I suppose you, and especially Sylvia and Nan, wonder sometimes how I am impressed one way or another with all these men always at hand. I remember Sylvia saying something about, "If Marcia does not find a husband over there, what chance do Nan and I have in the States?" She was joking, of course, because they would, or will never, have any trouble.
    Over here, I have not changed only that, since we see many people and that is our job, we find ourselves thinking and talking personalities. Always before, I seemed so sure of a direction in life, not exactly planned, but the long view was there and it kept me going. I had a God-given talent and I suppose I still have it.

When I meet and talk to someone who brings out the best in me, which is recognition of me as the whole person, it is comparable to playing a part well and thoroughly on the stage so that an audience sees the character in its entirety and so applauds. Here I have no script and, unless I feel a kindred spark in another person, It is harder to react spontaneously.

I think I am getting around to a point but it will take a lot of thinking before it becomes clear even to me. As I said before, this is a job of personalities and listening to people who are living and partly living in a world at war. Life is very real and yet not secure in the future. I often say, "What am I doing here? Am I really needed and am I serving any purpose?" I have no particular work to do. And yet I know that we are helping the war effort and we are appreciated.

This place is run with the most astounding lazy inefficiency you can imagine, but it does have a charming atmosphere that is felt by everyone. There is really nothing here for the guests to do, except swim, read, sleep (good hammocks for afternoon siestas), pump the Pianola, play Ping-Pong, eat and just sit and talk. The place runs smoothly. We have three good people on the staff who take a loving family interest in the place So much so, that it is they who are searching for further staff and getting it too.

If Arlene hasn't done the menu by 11:00 a.m., she'll ask me to take care of it. I was annoyed at first but I do not care now. She is always able to handle climactic situations. High-ranking officers love her. She chats on and on with them and makes a story out of the most mundane events, such as the time Mrs. Hayhoe, who weighs 220 lbs, fell down on top of three officers who were having a meeting. Mrs. Hayhoe was tiptoeing around their feet while she swept. She slipped and went down with a thundering crash that awakened Arlene from a sound sleep. I often hear her repeating anecdotes over and over until I detect the exact same wording as though memorized.

Marie and I take care of the little people who stay here. Marie is always jolly and sparkling. I suppose it gives officers a little more encouragement to see her. She certainly looks as though she would "give" more than I. She is very round, always dieting. She takes care of her beauty with all sorts of remedies in bottles. She even has an eye wash which may enhance the sparkle in her eye, I don't know. Nevertheless, I am American. One officer said yesterday that I am the only Red Cross girl he dares speak to and is sure of a response. I try to be responsive even if I do not always feel like carrying on a repartee. Another very nice officer said once, "You will make someone a good wife," and I said, "Why?" and he answered, "Because you have pleasing ways."

I have met only one or two officers that I would say excited me in any way. One was married, so I could not very well encourage my reactions in that sphere, and the other one is also a married man, but separated. Needless to say, I cannot encourage that, either, because how do I know?

COFFEE and SYMPATHY
World War II Letters from the Southwest Pacific

As a matter of fact, the latter case is something I do not feel I should consider a closed situation. I am enclosing a letter from him and you can take it for what it is worth.

He struck me with his sincerity. He is attractive, well-educated and charming with a love of adventure. This is proved by the variety of work he has tackled, including lumber jacking in Maine, writing for *Time* magazine and, at one time, singing with a top-notch orchestra. He graduated from Yale and lives in Hartford, Connecticut. His parents live in New York City. He and five other Navy boys of the nicest type came out here one day and loved the place. They were so happy just being here. They carried laundry, swept the ballroom, went swimming and just did nothing. At times like that this place becomes most significant. I noticed immediately that they were all married, a natural observation. The first night they were here I did not pay much attention to them. There were other people around to keep me busy. As the Navy officers were leaving, someone suggested they stay overnight and they did.

At breakfast next day I sat with them all and, for some reason or other, I was quite funny. They discovered I went to Bennington. It was Wednesday, dance-night and we had asked some townspeople for dinner to observe our respectable-dance and take the news back to the rest of the town. The Navy men stayed for the dance.

I still did not pay any particular attention to any one of them, but I noticed that Jim rather sought me. He was a good dancer, the 1934 variety. He was also sweet to the visiting firemen. He danced with the ladies and generally gave them a good time.

After the dance the Navy officers wanted to go swimming. Elaine and Arlene did not go but I did. I really did not want to go and get all wet and I certainly did not plan to get my hair wet. However, Jim said, "Get your hair wet." I decided it did not matter what I looked like so I did. Then he said, "My ex would never do this." I did not think anything about that. I did not even answer, certainly I did not think he said it for any particular reason, and I have seen the way some men carry on around here, so I just passed over the remark.

I talked with him on the beach or, rather, he did most of the talking. I did not fall for him and yet I enjoyed him very much. He was fun to laugh and talk with, talk about anything. Jim asked if I would write to him. He told me his wife was a beautiful girl, had been a Powers model, but she was no fun. They had tried to make a go of it for four years. They are still friends but the marriage is no longer a success. He said nothing romantic such as he has expressed in his letters but I would have been cold to it, I am sure, and certainly would not have believed him. Arlene said the next day that she had seen a picture of a Red Cross girl when his wallet fell open and he had said she is a wonderful girl but not much fun.

They came again the next night but I had taken the staff to the movies, so I only saw Jim for a few minutes after they came from swimming. I spoke to him alone and asked him to show me the picture of the other Red Cross girl. He showed me saying, "You do not believe me." It was a pretty girl in a volunteer Red Cross uniform. He said it was Jane, his wife. I am writing to him very simple, friendly, but fairly colorful, letters, and I suppose there is no harm in that. I am not in love with him but I probably could make myself. This way I feel very safe and do not think I can get hurt. I would not want to discourage something that might be quite right. Time will tell, I presume. I can learn a lot about him from his letters, and he about me. At least, it is fun getting his letters whether anything comes of it or not.

What do you think? I write you about it because I would talk to you about it if I were home. You may rest assured my feet are always on the ground, perhaps too much so but that is the way I am.

Save his letter and send it back, please.

Love and Merry Christmas and Happy New Year,
Marcia

COFFEE and SYMPATHY
World War II Letters from the Southwest Pacific

Temptations of the Heart

In one of my letters to my family I mentioned that temptations of the heart surrounded me all the time, and it would be well to be on guard. Believing that I was heeding this warning, I did what seemed right to me. I made no serious mistakes. My conscience, sensitivity, and good fortune were usually my only protection in dealings with the men I met overseas during the war. However, once in a while my heart alone was my guide and then fortune kindly intervened.

Whenever I said farewell to the brave men leaving Yorkies for Papua New Guinea and beyond, I had a vivid image of what they would be up against. I pictured men landing on beachheads in total darkness, constantly under fire, and then battling their way through pouring rain in jungle terrain so muddy that tanks bogged down in it. And I remembered the newspaper reports about the struggle to save Australia from invasion by the Japanese.

In the summer and fall of 1942, before I knew that in six months I would be going overseas with the Red Cross, the papers were full of the defense of Port Moresby. There was fear the Japanese would attack Australia. I read about the Kokoda trail over the Owen Stanley Mountains in Papua New Guinea. It led between Buna in the north and Port Moresby in the south, still controlled by Australia. The Japanese were preparing to seize this last Allied stronghold by attacking it from the north over the mountains and from the east along the coast. Next they would invade Australia, a few hundred miles directly south of Papua New Guinea.

The Kokoda trail was an ancient, single-file track of slippery mud and rock through steaming jungles or across treacherous heights where the peaks reach 13,000 feet. On the path almost vertical in places, the infantry troops were tortured by driving rains, mosquitoes, malaria, dysentery, shortage of food, heat and cold, with 70-pound packs, and always at the point of exhaustion.

The Aussies stopped the enemy just 32 miles from Port Moresby and forced them back north along the trail. The Japanese were met and conquered by the U.S. forces near the village of Buna, not yet reclaimed by the Allies. Australia was saved.

From my first days at Yorkies Knob there was a regiment of Amphibious Army Engineers stationed at Cairns. The officers came often to eat and relax at our club. There was a charming southern captain who was the first person to capture a bit of my heart. He always came with a group of his friends and after dinner we all chattered together or took turns playing Ping-Pong.

We both knew without a word expressed that our feelings for each other were very temporary, even insignificant. He had a beautiful wife whom he loved very much and I was a virtuous, lonely young woman who trusted the captain's treatment of me. He invited me to their officers' club dance in Cairns. It was great fun and in the car on the way home he put his arms around me and kissed me. He left me at the door of our club with a gentle "goodnight." The last time I saw him, a few days later, in late September, he came with his friends for dinner to say farewell before they left the next morning for the "hot" area in the north.

After dinner we went for a short walk along the beach and soon sat down on the sand. As usual the moon was shining over the sea. He carefully put his hand on one of my breasts, and held it there quietly for a few moments. This was not something that I knew much about. Then we arose and walked back to the club. I never saw him again, nor did he write and I certainly did not expect it. Just after the war ended he called me in New York City. He was under the impression that I had married and wanted us to have dinner with him and his wife.

Perhaps I should have realized then that I was not protecting myself from situations with men that might end unhappily. What happened to my early fears about entanglements with married men? I met hundreds of officers. Why couldn't I have appreciated the attentions of a nice single Navy lieutenant who liked me? What was the matter with me? Well, I was saved that time.

Soon after the captain left, I met Jim Wilder, a Navy lieutenant in the process of divorce. He stopped for a few days at Yorkies before leaving for New Guinea. He was just as I have described in my letters, a tall, handsome man, beautifully built with melting blue eyes, and a dazzling smile, who oozed charm and was a marvelous dancer. We went swimming in the evening, he kissed me afterwards and we agreed to write to each other.

Sometime after Jim Wilder's first friendly letters arrived, I saw a lot of an Australian colonel and an American Navy lieutenant who were stationed in Cairns. They were both married. One day, during a crowded Sunday lunch at Yorkies, I was waiting on table and carrying two desserts. Where to put down the dirty plates from the table? I caught the eye of the lieutenant. He was watching me. Aware of this audience, I quickly managed to hold the two puddings in one hand then, taking the empty plate from the diner, I smilingly placed it on the floor and served one pudding and, again glancing the lieutenant's way, happily went on serving. The lieutenant always came with the Australian colonel and we soon became a threesome. We had wonderful conversations and they came often for dinner.

The night in late January 1944 when the lieutenant finally had to leave the area, we were sitting in the semi-darkness at Yorkies Knob in front of the building. The generator had gone off and we had only kerosene lamps. The colonel had left for a moment. Without thinking of any consequences, just to let him know that I would miss him, I put the lieutenant's hand on my cheek where tears were rolling down. The lieutenant started to grab me and I pulled back. He said, "Marcia, remember I have feelings too." Then he led me into the darkness of a hallway and held me. At that moment the colonel returned. He called us. We were frozen in shock. He walked all around calling. We came forth.

The lieutenant left the next day but six months later I received a very short note from him signed Lt. Ferris. We always addressed our guests by their title and last name. He wrote that he would like to hear from me and about me. I was surprised to hear from him and hoped there was no change in his marriage. Yes, I had loved him, but I did not answer him. By this time, Jim Wilder was writing beautiful love letters and I was responding with all my heart.

It was not easy to remain aloof from officers who attracted me at Yorkies Knob and I was not particularly smart about men. There was nowhere to go and nothing to do but work and smile in the presence of all at the Knob. I chatted with everyone and dated many of the officers who visited the club, but I felt strongly attracted to only three. They all left. Jim Wilder wrote a few times in early December, and then I did not hear from him again until late February, when I was about to go on leave in Sydney.

While in Sydney I visited the Australian colonel and his wife at their home. He asked me about Jim and said he thought that our romance was serious. I told him about the hiatus between Jim's letters, and that I had been writing only newsy, friendly letters.

[Yorkies Knob]
December 23, 1943

Dearest Family,

Happy Anniversary, Mother and Dad! Did you have one?

Why not go and see a play now on me? Since the Officers' Club in town is having a dance both Christmas Eve and Night, we thought it best to concentrate on a homey atmosphere here at Yorkies, and plan for a good Christmas dinner. A few weeks ago we hauled out our meager collection of decorations — some leftovers and a few rolls of colored crepe paper I picked up in a little store while on a shopping tour one day last August. The red paper would make beautiful tiny baskets with handles. Each person would have one at his place filled with peanuts for Christmas dinner. We can always get plenty of those but they do not come shelled.

I collected my material — cardboard, scissors, glue, ruler, pencil and red paper. I started to work quite determinedly and soon an inquisitive colonel began watching me. He criticized my production, actually giving me helpful hints, and then he looked around to see if anyone was looking while he dared to compromise his manhood by pasting little boxes together. We made nearly 25 boxes that night.

The next night I started in again. I succeeded in getting another officer interested. The colonel of the night before said he was taking the night off. However, I was terribly lucky because one by one the officers gathered around the table. I would give one a pair of scissors and he would fringe the edges, another would paste, and some would make the handles. I insisted upon the latter and was gratified later to see many officers with their dates leave the dining room after Christmas dinner, swinging the little baskets on their fingers.

Finally, the same colonel stuck his head in the door. He gave us a few pointers on the production line, and then went outside for more recruits. I was a bit desperate for a moment because I was running out of implements for so many people. Everyone wanted to get in the swing shift. I then thought of the large stock of peanuts and put two naval officers to work on shelling them. One of the workers stood up for two hours and shelled and shelled. He did not even stop to sample an orange drink I had sent one detail to make. We brought the number of baskets up to 75 that night. I told them all to come back for the last 25 the next night and, to my pleasure, they were there and quite willing to snip and paste until the job was completed.

Monday night Arlene and I went again with two Navy men about 40 miles from here to an Italian family restaurant for dinner. The people are from the north of Italy — light hair, black eyes and smooth, olive complexions. Mrs. Di Giovanni can only serve eight or ten people at a time, and only caters to a few special customers. It is a small, wooden hotel right on the side of the road, certainly nothing very grand, but in this part of the country there are not any luxurious houses, and not many neighbors even in peacetime. This home is as clean as a whistle. She has beautiful white linens, even the embroidered white curtains always look as though they had just been washed and starched. She has silver and crystal, glasses for every kind of wine. It was really marvelous to see all the linen, silver, crystal and large white dinner napkins. Our escorts had made arrangements for us to have corsages of pink and white roses set at our places.

We had hors d'oeuvres, wine, spaghetti, vegetables, chicken, pineapple cream pie and champagne. Delicieuse! We came straight home afterwards because it was late. About three miles from Yorkies we got a flat tire. Thousands of mosquitos proceeded to chew us up, so we walked until a jeep came along and took us home.

The other night we were sitting out in front of the house. I went out to the kitchen to get some juice, when I heard Marie calling me quite violently. I came out and there was a small brown snake, a death adder, deadly poisonous, crawling around the curved trunk of the palm tree right where an officer had been leaning.

I have heard of these snakes but never had seen one. They are apt to come out in the wet weather and the rainy season has begun a bit. We still have a lot of sunshine but it rains most every night and sometimes during the day. It just pelts down.

So — the men beat the snake with a stick and killed it. Then they proceeded, as boys will do, to prop open its small mouth with matchsticks and then with tweezers to dissect the insides. The snake kept squirming and I felt sure someone would die. Then they went out and fed it to the chickens which we ate the next day for lunch. No ill effects yet, so I guess the poison dies with the snake. If it does nip you, there is not much hope. Apparently, they only attack you if bothered. Not long ago a woman was fatally bitten on a sidewalk in Cairns.

Next day — Tuesday. Arlene and I were invited to go on a small boat across a bit of water, about an hour's ride, to an aborigine mission. It was quite out of this world. No cars, of course. Wooden houses with thatched roofs. I do not know what they eat. I suppose they grow a lot, and perhaps some foodstuff is imported. There were very large turtles lying around, some weighing perhaps over 350 lbs. The aborigines had bought them from some small sailing craft manned by natives from the Solomon Islands.

The children were all gathered in the rec hall, a sideless, frame structure. Some of the children were beautiful — light hair, dark, smooth skin and blue eyes. They sang two Christmas carols for us and their harmony was amazing. Then we walked all over the village. We bought some feathered flowers and some red beads. A couple of little dark boys climbed way up a high coconut palm to get us some coconuts. Then they peeled them with their teeth; it was quite remarkable the way they yanked at that tough skin and then pulled it off. On the way home we saw the small sailing ships manned by the islanders with bright-red dyed, curly hair, and we bought a turtle. Each boat carried two pigs.

                                            Love,
                                            Marcia

Marcia Ward Behr

[Yorkies Knob]
December 29, 1943

Dearest Family,

    Yesterday I received Mother's V-mail written on the 16th. I guess that is about as fast as letters travel this way. I hate to tell you this, but no Christmas packages have arrived so far, except Aunt Mary's which came a month ago. They will come some day, I am sure.
    I know you had a merry Christmas and I was surprised to find that we had one too. We had quite a few people staying here, so it was a congenial gathering. I think I wrote you about making the Christmas baskets. A day before Christmas two large cartons from the Red Cross arrived chock full of colored crepe paper and little else but some cellophane tinsel. We decided to let our guests experiment individually or collectively, as they so desired, on the decorations. That may have been a mistake but everyone had fun. The spirit was there, although the result was more like a Slavic carnival than a white Christmas.
    Mrs. Hayhoe took charge upstairs and she had a detail of three or four officers cutting narrow strips of all colors. They twined the strips together and strung them across the upstairs porch ceiling. She made a big red bell with a silver tassel to hang in the middle and made multicolor curtains for the doors opening onto the porch.
    I had waited all day to go cut down the Christmas tree. Imagine going out into the woods and chopping down your own. Also, imagine Christmas in the tropics — summer clothes and just dying of heat every time you do anything energetic like moving from one chair to the next.
    I had to go to town in the morning and get tons of supplies to last from Friday night until Tuesday. Even the bakeries stay closed all that time. I did not get out here to Yorkies until 2 p.m. and then Arlene wanted to go to town for something. There was no other car to get the tree. Arlene did not leave until late afternoon, but one of our regular guests returned and he drove Ramon, the Filipino, me and two axes to chop down our Christmas tree. We drove about six miles to the edge of a river and there were some pine-looking trees, somewhat thin and scraggly, growing in the sandy soil. We looked about quite a bit and finally chopped down three large branches, planning to tie them together to make a full tree. We gathered separate branches for decorating and piled it all into the jeep and tooted home again.
    We actually had a very nice Christmas. We spent all Eve decorating the whole house. Each one expressed himself individually and it looked like it. I just stood around and let everyone else do the work. We put the trees in sand in large pots — which worked beautifully. We put branches all up and down the stairs

and in the lobby using crepe paper galore to brighten it up. We hung green paper wreaths on all the posts in the dining room and covered the same posts first with red crepe paper. Someone painted a huge Santa Claus on one wall in the dining room.

Someone else painted "Merry Christmas" on the large mirror with a big red bow overhanging. Streamers hung from one end of the room to the other. It was really gaudy. We put one tree in the ballroom and one in the lobby which we decorated with tinsel and Santa Clauses. We finished a little after midnight.

The little children around the place were very excited about the activities. They rushed around with strips of crepe paper decorating chairs and legs of tables and asking about Santa Claus. Poor little things! One cannot buy toys and dolls at all. I bought the little ones each a sunsuit. I tried to get all of the staff — about 12 people — each a little something. About 12:30 Christmas Eve we all refreshed ourselves with a cool drink and sat around talking until long after three. Then we went in swimming. Arlene had gone to the dance at the club and Marie went to midnight mass, so I was holding forth.

We had a marvelous swim and about five of us then watched the dawn come up. It was beautiful. I rarely get up that early. It was 7:30, so I just showered and dressed. Marie was still up, and we put the presents under the tree. Then Marie and I took a short nap.

We had breakfast and the staff came for "The Tree" and the opening of the presents. The little children were very excited. We all opened our gifts and then we sang carols around the tree and everyone was very pleased.

The rest of the day we just sat around, being too tired and it was too hot to do anything. We had decided to put on evening dresses for dinner. Arlene and I both wore bright green dresses and everyone oh'd and ah'd at us. I really felt I looked pretty well, only it certainly seemed strange to be in a long dress. We had a big turkey dinner. I filled all the little red baskets we had made with nuts and candy that people had given us. We had two big sittings and nearly a hundred people.

I went to the dance at the officers club afterwards which was rather a sad affair, since there had been a big dance the night before. I guess everyone was pretty tired. We came home early. I sat up and talked till about 2:30 when I went upstairs to bed. But I was hungry, so I got my flashlight and came down by myself to raid the icebox. I ate turkey and nuts and candy and cookies and then very happily went to bed.

I thought of all of you and what you were doing. Of course our Christmas came a day before yours, but it is all the same. I remember last Christmas night I went to the opera. Lots of

Love,
Marcia

Marcia Ward Behr

[Yorkies Knob]
Jan. 5, 1943

Dearest Family,

People are still getting Christmas packages so mine still may arrive. Our New Year's celebration was a bit like Christmas. The Officers' Club had a dance on the eve and the next night everyone was too tired to do anything. We did not plan any party. A few people were here. We all went to bed soon after midnight. I sat and talked politics to one person most of the evening.

I have been getting out in the sun a bit lately so I have a little tan again. I do not dare to go in swimming very far for fear of the sharks, but I am sure the salt water is good for me. At any rate I feel better when I exercise a bit. It is certainly hot here, not bad at Yorkies but in town I just perspire and perspire. It is disgusting.

John Wayne and his U.S.O. group have been staying here while in town. He is so tall that Mrs. Hayhoe had to get her husband to put an extension on the end of the bed for his overhanging legs. I have not talked to him much but he seems very nice. There is also a baritone, John Deloche, and two girls in the troupe. Yesterday morning, after they left, I got a telephone call. "Did you find John's teeth?" the man asked. I looked and looked for his two back teeth, but to no avail. He found them in his pocket, I am glad to say.

I went to the show last night. The Special Services have erected a huge tent with a stage and it is a good thing. It protects audiences from the searing sun and summer rains.

The performance was not bad, considering they had just received the script the day before and rehearsed it at Yorkies. The girls were not very beautiful but, then, almost anything goes when you do not see many shows. They sang new songs that we have not heard: "Sunday, Monday and Always" and "Pistol-Packin' Mama." Old stuff to you, I know. John Wayne had a few words to say, a few jokes and smiled his big smile. The girls had a dialogue, sang and played the accordion. People enjoy anything.

Love,
Marcia

[Yorkies Knob]
Jan. 14, 1944

Dearest Family,

Arlene has been sick for over a week. She really looks quite ill. It started with a slight cold. Actually, I think both she and I have been in this place long enough. I do not know how she feels about it, but those are my sentiments.

At any rate, the doctor suggested that Arlene go on leave — an excellent idea, I think. She has a responsible job and a tiring one. Marge Wood, now stationed at the Cairns club, and I will go on leave as soon as Arlene gets back. I hope nothing untoward happens because it would be nice to get away and have some time of my own and not have to act in any particular way or be agreeable if I do not feel like it.

With Arlene away, it will be hard for me to do everything myself but I have been doing it for a week anyway, so I guess I can continue. I did it once before when she was on leave.

By the way I received one package of a beautiful white silk blouse from Sylvia. I just adore it and want to wear it all the time. Perhaps the other things will come along. I do hope so. We have had three officers here spending their leaves. They have great fun squeezing orange and pineapple juice every night. I buy a crate of oranges every day and a dozen pineapples. There is nothing better than fresh pineapple juice. The fruit is unlike the ones you buy in the States. It is sweet and extremely juicy, not at all tart. It is an awfully messy job to squeeze them. You have to use your hands as well, but it is a good iced drink and one needs a lot of cold liquids in this heat. Boys from New Guinea say it is cooler there.

Last night was dance night again and we rather dread it. It really is a workout. The people who come now never come here any other time, so they really do not have the place at heart. One has to be a regular lady policeman and a diplomat. We try to keep people out of the icebox and from taking glasses, blankets [for the beach], squeezing fruit juices and anything else they fancy. They are pretty good about it, but, if you do not watch, things can get pretty out of hand. It is a strain and I hardly ever feel like dancing. I always have to put out the milk and cookies and clean up everything afterwards. At least no one else offers, so I do it. There are sometimes nice people around, whom I know, and they always help me. However, I will benefit by all this experience in the long run, I am sure.

I received your V-mail Christmas letter and Tom's letter. I shall write to him one of these days. I owe a lot of letters. I am very bad, but I need a new stimulus.

Love,
Marcia

Marcia Ward Behr

[Yorkies Knob]
January 29, 1944

Dearest Mother and Family,

This is dreadful. I sicken every time I think of how long it is since I have written to you or anyone. Not a letter have I written. A lot has happened and I know you must be anxiously waiting word.

First I want to thank you all from the bottom of my heart for all the wonderful Christmas presents that have finally arrived. Everything is perfect, the books, the blouse, the pajamas and the watch. A fine naval watch-maker adjusted the watch and it runs beautifully now. Thank you all. I am sure that the other packages will come soon.

As you know, Arlene has been sick for three weeks and I have been running the place in fact, if not in name. It is really quite a job to do it all by yourself. One consolation, no time to think — disadvantage, no time at all and, if time, no time alone, no room to yourself.

My main worry has been transportation. We only have one Pontiac pickup truck and it is in perfectly terrible condition. We just had to do something about it. The battery was simply dead, but a new battery did not help much because something always wore it down in no time. Parts are difficult to get and the Army simply does not supply us with any good transportation. One day I took the car into the motor pool in the morning and told them about the battery. They sent me somewhere else. An old battery was finally discovered there and put in the truck. (The gear does not go in second and, when put in first, it is often in third and vice versa. The universal knocks. The truck needed a new generator and the voltage control was all off. The starter seldom worked and so I needed a push every time to start the old thing.) I change the tense of the verbs, because, for the time being at least, some of the complaints have been corrected.

At any rate, they fooled around with the battery, painted a new number on the car and, after waiting nearly two hours, the car was running and I started forth. I stopped first for gas and, naturally, I turned off the engine. Well, it never started again. I was desperate. It was Monday — quartermaster day — huge weekly supplies to be collected. I called Arlene and she told me to call the transportation officer. Within the space of five minutes Arlene and I and a major all called the transportation officer. I guess he felt obliged to do something. He told me to wait and some vehicle would come. I waited nearly in tears. It was so hot and I was hungry and thirsty.

COFFEE and SYMPATHY
World War II Letters from the Southwest Pacific

Finally, I went to the Red Cross for lunch and waited some more. About two o'clock a two-and-a-half-ton truck, battered, shaking and very noisy, drove up with a driver. I was awfully mad and took it out on the driver a bit I am afraid. I resented being driven around. I knew we needed a car of our own way out at Yorkies. However, we went around and picked up supplies, including two 44-gallon drums, one of kerosene and another of oil.

Mrs. Jeffery, one of the cooks, had ridden into town with me and I told her to meet me at 4:30. We were through long before that and had to wait around for her, which did not help my disposition any, but at last we started out for home. We got just so far and the old truck sputtered and died right by the side of the road, but gratefully near the motor pool.

I was in great despair as the meat was already smelling and the milk was getting warmer and, in an open truck with the hot sun beating down on it, I had visions of a great food spoilage.

Soon a truck came and towed us back to the motor pool where they dickered for at least another twenty minutes trying to decide what truck could be used, or perhaps, what truck could make the trip. And then, of course, a great transfer of supplies had to be made.

I remember some soldier during the day stated that I did not look very happy. I laughed and remembered that our job is to keep smiling.

I stopped for our laundry (now being done by a lame man who boils the clothes outside in a big iron kettle over a fire and irons them the old-fashioned way) and decided the basket of laundry must go in front or blow to the universe in back. So, I made room by hopping into the back of the truck with no sides and no roof and stood up facing front, hanging on to the fuel drums and rode with the hot wind drying me off for the first time that day. Even if I could not laugh at the day's proceedings, at least I could appreciate the incongruity of my position.

As I write I am listening to Liszt's Hungarian Rhapsody. It is very pleasant. People tried to persuade me to go to the dance at the club tonight, but I have been longing to write to you. I really love to write home, but I like to have time and to be alone. I am sitting upstairs and they are playing the records outside in front of the house.

I had a bit of an ordeal a few minutes ago. A large number of Australian soldiers surrounded the ballroom. I came out and talked to them. Inside the ballroom there were officers playing Ping-Pong and the player-piano, but they left and the soldiers quite naturally took over. I knew if I did not do something, great multitudes would appear and then I would be swamped. I finally screwed up my courage and went into those who were playing the Pianola and said quite frankly that I thought they had better go because soon more soldiers would come and I would find it hard to handle the situation. They were very understanding and left at once. I was relieved. One feels quite helpless at such times. They could have laughed and made scornful remarks and just hung around. I don't like to be tough and I would hate to ask rank to appear and cause feeling.

I got a ride into town the next day with my bread baskets. I had been promised a vehicle for the day. I called the motor pool and waited out in front of the Red Cross with my baskets on the steps beside me. After some time a driver drove up in a jeep. Of all things! I cannot put supplies in a jeep. I think they thought by shopping I meant for pins and needles and lipstick. I sent the driver right back for a truck. As I sat waiting by the baskets, I felt very pathetic and some officers commented upon it just as my truck drove up. I hopped in and went to transport headquarters and put my helpless case before them. I told them I just had to have a car of my own. I knew it was necessary to make another trip that day for ice, and I needed something better than a scooter or a bicycle. I got some action. The transportation officer lent me his weapons carrier. Golly, but I was happy to feel the grip of the wheel again and, believe me, I had to grip that thing. Just give me any old truck, I can drive it now. The speedometer got stuck a couple of times which terrified me, but I learned to manage that. I was happy in my proprietorship.

Sunday our own pickup truck was delivered to us. It still stalled and had to be pushed by the guests in the morning and by anybody in town. However, I clung to it until the other day when they fixed the voltage control. Now it only stalls once in a while. Of course, the second gear is still bad and the universal knocks again, but I do not care.

As you know I have been waiting to go on leave. I am waiting for Marjorie Wood to take hers with me. In my next letter I shall tell you more on this subject.

Love,
Marcia

[Yorkies Knob]
Feb. 2, 1944

Dear Mother and Family,

I am pretty tired. I went to bed about midnight leaving the lights for an officer to turn out. Marie finally came up about two o'clock. I had not been asleep at all and the lights were still on. Marie said the officer was going to read awhile. It is not right to have the lights burning so late. Some guests might be disturbed by the light and the noise from the engine is anything but soothing. I waited a bit and then in desperation I got up and went down and put them out myself. I do not relish going out on these dark rainy nights. Too many big toads and maybe even snakes.

In my last letter I told you about the transportation difficulties and also mentioned the fact that Arlene was sick. She is such a weird personality. Perhaps I have been unfair to her in some of my remarks, but I have always reserved that I admire her sometimes. However, to me, she seemed too scheming a person for us ever to be good friends.

You may observe that I am writing in the past tense about Arlene. She had a cold and she remained confined to her room for over a week, sick and partly sick. A doctor came to see her and told her she needed a leave. I told her to take it ahead of me, though she has had one other long leave and three days just recently. However, I was the well one.

Before Arlene left, a telegram came from Area Headquarters saying they were sending a girl to keep me company while Arlene was away. A new person is company but even that is taking a chance on personalities. She can be a responsibility and a liability in a place like this, at least until she works into things which takes time.

Jane Randolph arrived the day after Arlene left and she was a great surprise and a relief, a lovely girl from Virginia, sweet, pretty, intelligent and a perfect lady.

I wish she could stay on here. Everyone liked her. She has not an unusual or terribly colorful personality, but she would wear forever. She was willing to do anything for me, but she had been quite sick, so I just let her relax and talk to the guests or go swimming when and if she felt like it.

Last Wednesday I was in town and I really got a shock. I think Jane, the new girl, was with me. Someone said there was a Red Cross woman to see me. She came out and it was Marge Fowler, the new club director of Yorkies Knob. News to me. I cannot say I am exactly hurt that Arlene did not tell me. We had had a discussion over something that was none of her business and I frankly told her then that I did not like her too much.

I also told her that I knew what she could say to the Red Cross officials about me. She could too, though it would not be true. It would be my word against hers and they think she has done a simply marvelous job here. I do not belittle what she has done but the place is a natural. For her age and experience she has done very well and I would not have wanted to have been in her shoes. However, that is not the way to judge things. You cannot make allowances for people's failings all the time. One does not see a play and say, "That was very good considering the director has never done anything before."

For a long time we have had an engineer with a wooden leg and an old Filipino, Ramon, to do all the work about the place: clean out the grease traps and icebox, get and chop the firewood, take care of the chickens, unload the truck, all the general outside jobs. Ramon has been practically incapacitated since he lugged the heavy logs for firewood. I told Arlene before she left that she would have to get someone to empty the garbage every night at least, because I knew Ramon would be going to the hospital. She told me that she gave me no authority to hire anyone while she was away. A ridiculous thought. What if the whole staff left while she was away.

Arlene went to the Army Engineers before she left to ask them to come and make some improvements. Since then I have been reminding them and quite a bit has been repaired. I took Ramon to the hospital the day Arlene left. He has T.B. and heart trouble. Our main waitress left because of sickness the next day. We went right to work to try and hire replacements. It is now two weeks later and we are getting help. I say "we" because the present staff has made all the suggestions. They are wonderful. Arlene made the remark that her job is to look after the staff. Actually, they look after us.

Feb. 6 — Apparently Arlene has been planning to transfer since January 1. I think she wants to go north.

A week almost has passed since I started this. Things have been going quite smoothly. I am most happy about the new chicken house. We have had a couple of boys detailed from the Army and they have built a new chicken house. They tore down the verminated, smelly old one, extended the runs and separated the roosters, ducks, etc., from the hens, so they can feel free to lay some eggs.

Our new director, Marge Fowler, tells me tonight that she wants to go home and is writing a letter to that effect. I wish they would close this place. I would either like to go home or go somewhere else and try some real service work.

I do appreciate all your letters and will write soon.

                                          Love,
                                        Marcia

[Yorkies Knob]
Feb. 10, 1944

Dearest Family,

Just received your marvelous letter giving me some of your deep wisdom. I do get saturated with thoughts of unimportant things sometimes and they do bother me. I should work more consistently toward a greater understanding of the real existence and I would be a more progressive, peaceful, happier and wiser person. I lose track of any objective at times and it is, of course, then that I should cling harder than ever to thoughts of goodness and not let momentary, meaningless connections frustrate me. Sometimes one even forgets to hope.

Right now nothing is happening here. I shall try to use this dull time constructively. Something will happen soon. The supervisors know that I want and need a leave.

I am delighted that Joe Flynn called you. He is a very nice boy and he, with others like him, were here a lot. I saw a picture of the girl to whom he is engaged. She was very sweet and pretty.

I decided I had better write letters every once in a while to Jim. I know he would be writing if he could and he would want to hear from me.

Our chicken yard is a joy now. The little chicks are so happy — the roosters in their own quarters and the hens in their lovely new home. They have individual straw boxes and seem to be competing with each to lay more eggs. Production has gone up 100%.

It is candlelight again, so it is hard to see well. The rain just poured down tonight and came in the doors and windows before we could shut them all. I got sopped just shutting the front door. The rain pounds on the tin roof and I could scream and shout and sing and never compete with the noise it makes. I tried it, so I know.

Lots of love,
Marcia

[Yorkies Knob]
Feb. 13, 1944

Dearest Family,

Just like the tropics, it is raining. All day long it has rained with slight intervals of bright hot sunshine. I looked at my pallor in the mirror this morning and, remembering how healthy and brown I looked a month ago, I jumped into my suit for a sunning. The beach looked dry and the day bright. I stopped for a brief conversation and by the time I got downstairs clouds had encompassed everything. I gave up.

I called to see if the ice cream had come in on the train and, since it hadn't, I must make a trip to town to get some from another source. This latter is not so good, but ice cream on a Sunday is a tradition, so I needs must produce same. We had planned the usual chicken dinner and were attempting to enhance it with banana splits. We always try to have watermelons on hand too, just in case all else fails.

Friday night four of us, Marge Fowler and two officers were sitting upstairs reading. It was raining again, and we were alone. I was reading a Chekhov short story out loud. A Navy lieutenant walked upstairs to see me. He sat a moment and then went to the washroom. He came back almost immediately and said in a sly, calm way, "There is a visitor in the john." We followed him and, sure enough, high over the plumbing on the louvers was a two-foot, thin, brown snake, still but alert. Marge exploded and I worked myself up because it was surely a death adder. The men, particularly the Navy boy, were very unexcited, We screamed, "Kill it!" But they were nonchalant.

Sometime back there had been news of a woman who was walking on a sidewalk in Cairns. She was bitten in the ankle by a death adder. She ran screaming down the street and apparently died before anyone could help her.

Marge ran downstairs and came up with much equipment — shovel, rake, broom and other garden implements. Tom, the Navy boy, took the shovel and went after the snake. It was in an awkward place and up so high. I kept telling him to be careful. Might be instant death if it snapped. I had to run away when I saw Tom lift the shovel and hit the snake, and the adder (I still think it was one) raised up and stretched down the shovel almost to the killer's hand. I ran screaming for Marge.

After some time the brave boys came out to the sitting room where we were breathlessly waiting. They had made a thorough job of slaughtering the evil thing. Tom saved himself just in time by bashing the shovel, with the snake entwined, hard against the toilet seat. Sad results for our new plumbing which lay shattered like Dresden china.

Later on in the evening, when Tom was leaving, I went out to the car which he was having trouble starting. He was tinkering with the engine, drying off the spark plugs and distributors, etc. I stood by thinking about the trouble I would undoubtedly have in the morning with our truck. I felt my hair damp and stringy, hanging down my neck. I put my hand up and thought how unattractive and straight my hair was. As I took away my hand, I looked down and, in an instant, I saw it was not my hair but some horrible tremendous, black spider with many long legs that I had been caressing. I shuddered violently as I pushed it off and jumped up and down a couple of times, most happy, however, to find it was not my own hair.

I hope you are not affected by these horror stories, but I am only writing about what has been happening around here lately.

Much love,
Marcia

COFFEE and SYMPATHY
World War II Letters from the Southwest Pacific

[Yorkies Knob]
Feb. 21, 1944

Dear Family,

    I just received a present of a beautiful streamlined Eversharp pen. What with new paper and now a brand new shiny maroon and gold fountain pen, I have no excuse for not writing. There have been some nice Navy boys around lately and one of them, named Tom, gave me the present. He and a friend were here for dinner.
    It was Sunday and we had an unusually large crowd.
    I started to work in the kitchen about 5:30. I cut up and made the chicken salad and helped with the servings. We are really quite short-handed in the kitchen. As Marie and I were dishing out the ice cream, in came Owen and Tom. Marie had to go collect money from departing guests and I took charge of the volunteers. Tom dished out the ice cream and fruit salad. I gave Owen a towel and he and I wiped the dishes as fast as we could, so the girls (just two) could set up for the second sitting. Then a couple of more officers made the mistake of walking in and I had towels ready for them because, of course, they offered assistance.
    It has been raining a lot lately. It rains hard as anything for hours and dribbles and then suddenly drops down again — enough to throw you out of bed from the noise. Both Marge and I woke up last night as it crashed down on the roof. I am glad I came here when it was winter. The climate was delightful and then three months of steaming, hot, sunny and humid heat. Now the rains have come.
    I do not know whether I wrote that Charlotte Cooper is now the club director instead of Marge, who wants to go home. I really think now she is sorry she put her foot out so quickly and would like to stay on here.
    The old car would not go at all, so we got a ride into town and they gave us another old pickup. On the way home I heard a loud bumping noise and I put on the brakes to stop the car and ended up in a ditch. The wheels went lopsided. I backed the car out and drove it home slowly. The spring under the back wheel broke and now we are in the market for another car. I drove the thing in the next day. Having no car, we had to again call on a guest to carry over the laundry. Tom was willing and he carried the three bags down into his jeep and took them over.

Tom and Owen were here Friday night and Marie and I and the boys went for the laundry. We picked it up and drove on to the officers' club. The bar was closed, as it was after nine. We managed to find some lukewarm water to drink and danced a little. Then we drove into town and called on Marge Wood. She gave us some beer and we sat around until midnight and then drove home because we had to turn out the lights.

Joe Flynn was right about having to work around here. We are quite dependent on our guests. Joe is a darling boy. No, you are right, he has nothing to do with Jim Wilder. I still see some of the boys with whom Joe used to come out here. They are all very nice and we used to have fun. Every Sat. night for a while we would have a fire on the beach, eat hot dogs and drink beer supplied by the Navy, of course. I meant to tell you Joe might call you up. And, by the way, an enlisted man named Rocque (Rocky) is going home soon. He lives in New York City and I asked him to go see you.

At long last I received three letters from Jim Wilder, one was dated Dec. 22, not stamped until Feb. 6. He said his letters would be delayed because he was in a "hot area" and they are only allowed so much poundage of mail to come out every day. I am very glad I kept writing him because he does count on it a lot. I should write him more often, I guess, because he is really very serious.

I am pretty definitely going on leave next week. I heard rumors that the Red Cross is thinking of organizing traveling theatrical units. I shall look into that.

All my love,
Marcia

COFFEE and SYMPATHY
World War II Letters from the Southwest Pacific

Marcia Ward (Behr) World War II

Marcia Ward (Behr) Feb., 1943

These US Red Cross workers soon settled down after their arrival in Australia. Marion Prather, of Alabama, Marcia Ward and Ann Stevenson, of New York, gather around for a sing-song with guitar player, Peggy Armstrong.

Arrival in Brisbane - April 1943

Marcia and Arlene - Summer 1943

COFFEE and SYMPATHY
World War II Letters from the Southwest Pacific

Yorkies Knob - 1943

Elaine   Marcia   Arlene

On the beach at Yorkies Knob

COFFEE and SYMPATHY
World War II Letters from the Southwest Pacific

Marcia goes to Green Island on the Barrier Reef

Marcia on Green Island

COFFEE and SYMPATHY
World War II Letters from the Southwest Pacific

Marcia with Rita and two Filipinos

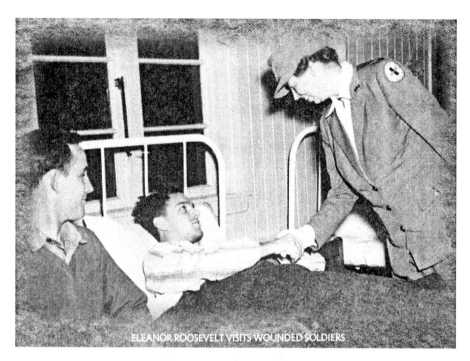

The army builds us a chicken coop

COFFEE and SYMPATHY
World War II Letters from the Southwest Pacific

The star looked a lot younger in 1943

Marcia outside the Mission House in Oro Bay, New Guinea - Sept., 1944

COFFEE and SYMPATHY
World War II Letters from the Southwest Pacific

Marcia and Theo visit a Negro regiment at Oro Bay, New Guinea, Sept., 1944

B 25 Bombers fly over Biak - November 1944

Our tent - Biak, November 1944

Mary Ellen, Charlie and Marcia check out

COFFEE and SYMPATHY
World War II Letters from the Southwest Pacific

Marcia smiles for a picture at the Biak Airport.

Marcia in the Jeepmobile

Marcia Ward Behr

View from our tent on Biak

COFFEE and SYMPATHY
World War II Letters from the Southwest Pacific

Marcia on the point just below the tent

Marcia Ward Behr

Mary Ellen, Marcia, Charlie and Marge with friends in front of our tent

COFFEE and SYMPATHY
World War II Letters from the Southwest Pacific

Charlie, Mary Ellen and Marcia near our tent

Mary Ellen Evans, Marcia Ward, Charlie Townes, Marge Shirley

COFFEE and SYMPATHY
World War II Letters from the Southwest Pacific

Marge, Marcia, Charlie and Mary Ellen

Marcia Ward Behr

The band for the Army Review in Biak November 1944

COFFEE and SYMPATHY
World War II Letters from the Southwest Pacific

Mary Ellen sings for the troops in her parachute gown

Clyde Carter and Muriel O'Connor with Marcia Ward as Granny in *Sparkin'*

COFFEE and SYMPATHY
World War II Letters from the Southwest Pacific

Granny Sparks gets her picture taken

Marcia Ward Behr

The 90th Bomb Group watches *Sparkin'* in the rain

COFFEE and SYMPATHY
World War II Letters from the Southwest Pacific

The children are given candy on the island of Japen

Marcia Ward Behr

THE WHITE HOUSE
WASHINGTON

September 25, 1943

Dear Mrs. Ward:

    I had the pleasure of meeting your daughter Marcia on my trip to the South Pacific and I know you will be glad to hear that she looked well and is enjoying her work.

    I was interested to hear from her that we have mutual friends in Mr. and Mrs. George Carlin.

        Very sincerely yours,

        Eleanor Roosevelt

Mrs. Roosevelt at Cairns, Beach Landing Is Staged

U. S. Troops Give Demonstration of Lae Tactics

By Wireless to the Herald Tribune
Copyright, 1943, New York Tribune Inc.

CAIRNS, Australia, Sept. 11. — Mrs. Eleanor Roosevelt arrived here today by plane from Rockhampton, 600 miles to the south, and saw at an American camp elaborate demonstrations of beach landing operations similar to those undertaken near Lae, New Guinea. She told members of her party that it was one of the most interesting demonstrations she had ever seen.

On the staffs of American Red Cross clubs visited by Mrs. Roosevelt today were: John A. McVickar jr., of 172 East Ninety-fifth Street, New York, director of the main club Cairns; Marcia Ward, 122 East Eighty-second Street, New York, staff assistant at the hostel where Mrs. Roosevelt arranged to pass the night, and Benedict de Angelo, of Oneonta, N. Y., one of the field workers operating out of Carins.

Cairns, in the tropical northeastern state of Queensland, is only a few hours flying distance from the bitterly-fought New Guinea front.

COFFEE and SYMPATHY
World War II Letters from the Southwest Pacific

Brisbane, July 3, '44

Presented by The American Red Cross

Lt. John B. Bryan Jr., writes to his wife at 122 Oak Street from somewhere in the South Pacific, he is now in New Guinea, about the hospitality and comforts of a Red Cross rest home.

"Several of us," writes Lt. Bryan, "spent Saturday night and Sunday at the Red Cross rest home, relaxing completely and enjoying ourselves. The atmosphere, hos-

LT. JOHN B. BRYAN, JR.

pitality, and food are all wonderful and we thoroughly enjoyed it all. We have been eating dinner there every night. It is like a little bit of home way over here. Miss Marcia Ward of New York City is one of the hostesses. She is young and pretty and very nice—it seems so good to see an American girl again."

Geneva, New York

In The Service
About The Boys From Our Town

SUNDAY MIRROR MAY 30 1943

Staff Sgt. Paul Wygodsky, 1154 Ward Ave., Bronx, has been appointed to the Army Air Force Administrative Officer Candidate School on recommendation of his commander at the Salt Lake City Air Base.

Pvt. Vincent J. Kramer, 328 E. 197th St., has been graduated as an aircraft mechanic at Seymour Johnson Field, N. C. ... 2nd Lt. Benjamin Kimlau, 101 Park St., has been graduated as a twin-engined plane pilot at Columbus, O., Army Flying School...Frederick London, 960 Park Ave., has been commissioned a lieutenant, as was Haley Fiske, 2nd, of 16 E. 98th St.

Salvatore Lisi, 49 Oak St., has been promoted to a staff sergeant at Patterson Field, Fairfield, O. ...Ellsworth Moats, 573 Jackson Ave., now is a master sergeant, and Ralph Parone, 1807 Archer St., is a corporal.

Aviation Cadet   Marcia Ward
Murray Fuchs   Red Cross

Jacob M. Trager, 1255 Grant Ave., has been made a staff sergeant at the Los Angeles Port of Embarkation...2nd Lt. Jacques Mayer, 670 West End Ave., is now assigned to the 11th Armored Division, Camp Polk, La. ...Philip Brosnan, 1714 Third Ave., and Stephen Cammarata, 197 Irving Ave., both machinists' mates, have been sent to special service schools at the Great Lakes Naval Training Station.

Cadet Murray R. Fuchs, 3554 Rochambeau Ave., has been rated one of the outstanding aviation cadets at Blackland Army Air Field, Tex...He is in a competition with six other cadets, one of whom will be chosen by ballots cast by women aircraft workers at the Cessna Aircraft Co., to accompany the outstanding women aircraft worker at Cessna when she visits the field June 25-26.

Hugh Toner, 401 E. 136th St., is taking ground course training at the AAF center, Southwestern College, Memphis, before embarking as an aviation cadet...Auxiliary Madeleine Roenne, 340 Mosholu Parkway South, is in a special course in WAAC Administration at East State Teachers' College, Tex...One of her classmates is Doris Ginsberg, 810 Hunts Point Ave.

Third Officer Theodora Cimberg, 155 E. 75th St., has been assigned to the Washington and Lee Special Service School... Auxiliary Bertha Stein, 237 E. 54th St., is at Fort McCain, Miss. ...Three New Yorkers were among the aviation machinists' mates graduating from the training school at Great Lakes Naval Base; Harry Schrater, 244 E. Seventh St.; Louis Reuter, 171 W. 71st St., and Joseph Maynulet, 640 W. 139th St.

Marcia Ward, 122 E. 82nd St., is a Red Cross staff assistant now on duty in Australia.

Marcia Ward Behr

[Sydney]
End of Feb., 1944

Dearest Family,

    Amazing, I am on my leave! Marge and I got a plane ride out of Cairns last Friday morning and landed in Sydney early in the afternoon of the same day. Remarkable, when you think it took me four days and nights to cover the same distance by train going to Cairns nearly ten months ago.
    I am pretty determined to ask for a transfer now, though I have no thoughts as to where I would like to be sent up north. That seems to be where everyone is. It is too far away from everything down here. I should have that experience.
    I suppose Hilda (Hilda Thompson, recently Red Cross director of the Cairns area) has probably come to see you and told you a lot about the area. Yorkies Knob must be more vivid now. She could also describe New Guinea to you. Sometimes I hesitate in wanting to go there, not merely on account of the food and living conditions but because of the abnormality of the life. All those men living away from the civilization we know. A handful of girls up there amongst millions of men. Does Hilda think we accomplish a great deal? Canteen work might be important providing they can get supplies and equipment. We would just be a hindrance in the really forward areas and the front lines are pretty intangible.
    I have been talking to a Red Cross worker who has been on the stage for twenty years. She contends that recreation is bound to be slim up there. There is not much you can do. Certainly sports are planned by the field workers. There may be small huts with books and writing material, lukewarm lemon drinks or coffee — maybe.
    If they send up any performers, they have got to be super: Ray Bolger, Joe E. Brown or Bob Hope. Just a pretty girl, an ordinary torch singer, is more of a flop than a morale-builder. Something, or someone really funny in a big way, is what it takes. This Red Cross worker thought that perhaps groups of soldiers doing their own stuff and touring from camp to camp, would be more feasible than what they are, apparently, doing in England. Small, unknown professional units would work over there but it is an entirely different situation up north.
    Thinking it over, though, I would rather go north than be sent any other place around here.

                                                   Love,
                                                 Marcia

[Sydney]
March 7, 1944

Dearest Family,

I was in Brisbane and had quite a good time. We took a little travel time. Some of it we spent at a beach resort to try and cure our colds. Marge Wood comes from Washington. She is not exactly my type, but an attractive girl. She is a good person with whom to spend a leave.

While in Brisbane we were both pretty busy. We went everywhere there was to go. I gained an appetite and drank enough beer to put on some weight. I really look well again so that people down here who have not seen me for ten months, say, "My, you look well, your work must agree with you." I do not look strained or tired anymore. In fact I feel very happy.

I went to the A.R.C. office in Sydney almost immediately and found six letters from home including one from Daddy. Also a letter from Jim Wilder and one from a friend in New Guinea. It was too marvelous! Such good news for all of you.

I am not so sure about New Guinea or whether they would send me there. Jim wants me to try and come near him, but I do not think that would be such a good idea either. He really and truly seems to love me. How he can be so sure on such a short acquaintance, I do not know. I may love him for all I know, but his intentions had better be honorable. He sounds sincere but one never knows and I am not counting on anything that may not exist.

Nan wants advice about joining A.R.C. I have avoided this moment because I do not know what to say. She has read my letters and must realize the disappointments and disillusionments as well as fun or glamour, if any. It has been a most marvelous experience for me. It is sometimes a strain and one gets lonely and one could easily do something that would never happen at home. Men are affected in more ways than one by the war. They are far away from home too. The life is not regular or normal and one naturally tries to adjust and keep happy. Our work is a bit intangible and becomes a game of personalities and people. It may be different in another theater of war, but I imagine it is the same the world over. Nan is young but she is good, intelligent, practical, mature and of a happy disposition. She is also very attractive which, in a way, is a leveler in this game. She would keep her feet on the ground, I am sure, but it is a big step and, if she finds a good, satisfactory job at home in which she can be happy and she has friends and a tangible security, it might be better. I do not know. I cannot advise.

I am delighted to hear that my college debt is just about paid up. Do not wear yourself out, Mother. See if you can get some more help.

All my love,
Marcia

Marcia Ward Behr

[Sydney]
March 12, 1944

Dearest Family,

I am trying to see and do everything while on leave. As a matter of fact I am getting around to the night spots fairly well and, for once in my life, I am going with just anybody because actually there is no one I know very well here in town. Marge Wood found that the three officers she knew on the ship coming over are here, and so we have dates. Mine was a fat colonel who could not keep time and wanted to dance every dance. First we went to a symphony concert. That was good. It was marvelous to hear some music again and I did not have to talk or listen to anyone.

I was terribly annoyed with my hair. The day before yesterday I got a permanent and you know that I usually rush home and take drastic measures to redo the set. Well, I did not have time to do anything about it until yesterday afternoon at 4:30. We were going out for dinner at 6:30. I washed my hair and Marge said to let her try to fix it for me. Reluctantly I let her do it. She gave me a very severe upsweep. Everyone said they liked it, but I did not. Our dates came and out I went. I suddenly thought, "Well, nobody knows me and, if they do, they won't recognize me." Thank goodness my date was somebody I never hope to see again.

The nicest officer I have seen here was one I bumped into in the hotel while eating lunch with Marge. First, I must tell you that Arlene is here. All is friendly and pleasant. I went out with her the other night on a double date. Well, Arlene was having lunch with Pete Motto, whom I know too. I went over to ask them something and saw three other officers that we all knew. Marge came over and we finished lunch with them. They are quick on the trigger and gentlemen. They have asked us to go to the Russian music festival and one also asked me to go to a production of *The Pirates of Penzance* tomorrow night. When I came home, I found roses from him with a card saying not to forget Monday. That is encouraging. Yesterday Marge and I went to a surf carnival like the tournaments at Jones Beach. That was fun and there was a big beautiful surf and it was a wonderful clear day and our seats were the best.

I do not think I want to go back to Yorkies Knob. I feel sure it may close soon anyway. New Guinea is the most tempting probably because I know what the clubs and places are like on the mainland and there is no mystery left. Also, it is autumn here now and my hands are cold all the time.

All love,
Marcia

COFFEE and SYMPATHY
World War II Letters from the Southwest Pacific

[on leave in Sydney]
March 16, 1944

Dearest Family,

I received more mail from you yesterday and a letter from Jim Wilder. I am glad I had my mail forwarded to Sydney. There was a nice letter from Nan and a V-mail from Mom.

The other night Marge and I went to dinner at a night club and then to a concert of Russian music including Tchaikovsky's Pathetique symphony which was excellent, I thought. Then we all went dancing afterward. Every place is terribly crowded and you must book ahead. You have to bring your own liquor and then buy setups and pay for a dinner whether you eat it or not. It seemed glamourous and quite metropolitan.

The Pirates of Penzance was excellent; a fine comedian played the General. As a matter of fact I enjoyed it as much as any G. & S. I have ever seen. Perhaps because I am starved for theatrical entertainment.

I have been going out most of the time with an officer I met just once or twice in Cairns. He is Czech and quite nice but not very exciting. I get him to tell me all about Czech history and then he does all the talking. He tells me about New Guinea too, quite cold-bloodedly. No secrets, of course, but it is horrible what those men go through and still come out laughing.

Yesterday I went by ferry to a beach resort to visit an Australian major and his wife. I knew him in Yorkies Knob. It was a beautiful day, quite cool but I was warm in my winter suit, and I had a lovely time talking with them.

I suppose you are curious about the Jim Wilder development. He is very sincere and something tells me that it is right. How can I not love someone who writes:

Marcia Dearest,
  Note the pressure, but please stand by. Kinda been thinking about you all the time and want to shove all the Army chaps aside for the moment because I cannot be there with you and defend my rights. And besides, I want to tell you that a guy who never washes his own clothes too well, whose hair is practically ingrown, who has grown to adore chlorinated water just wants you to know that he, even now, loves you and wants you to use that love to lean back on and utilize in every way so that whatever you do you will always know that he is there with you and

respects you in every way and wants you to love him no matter where you go or no matter just what you are doing.

As you can readily scan he is much afeared of your tooting about said Australia and thereon and would rather have you with him so that he can share your major tribulations and, above all, he wants you to know that he is scared of some gent in "blues" or khaki who might take over. How that "green fellow" gets up this far to annoy people, I really don't know!

So, Marcia, I just want you to understand that all you are doing is a part of us all and we all count on you. But just every now and then there is present one person who is with you in everything and who prays for you to keep it up and who wants everything said on one beach to continue for all time. I am not ashamed for having written this, Dear. It is there for you to accept and to have. One thing being that here there are no temptations and so one can think of a cove rather clearly and in that please know that I do love you ... Jim.

I can love him, I know that. Never fear, though, everything will work out for the best. I am not closing my eyes to other men. I see plenty but I certainly do not get interested in any of them. You know me, though — hard to please. I explained to Marjorie about Jim. She is wary of such things because she actually joined the Red Cross to get away from someone who was married and kept putting off a divorce. She said he sounds like a marvelous person and intelligent. So, I am sure he would not lead me on for nothing. What can it get him, unless he is a sadist which I know he is not?

You asked me where he comes from in the U.S. He gave his address in our guest book at Yorkies as New York City and his identification tag says, Hartford, Conn.

Ann Lalli and I had our palms read this afternoon. Funny, it was just after I had written Jim that I did have faith in him and that we must expect the best of the future. I saw no use in holding doubts any more. I told him I was afraid of being hurt and, in thinking of myself, I never considered that he is taking a risk in getting hurt too. I know he is wondering all the time whether he will lose me. After all I am surrounded by a few men most of the time. He said, "You sound rather uncertain about your feelings toward me and I can understand the reason. But, will you please accept all verbatim until I can actually prove to you that I am sure of my love for you and am very sincere. Naturally, being away from you, I can't help feeling that I might lose you, dear. I really don't ever want that to happen and I constantly pray that it will not. You must have lots of faith in me, Marcia. I count on you so very much that it would be terrific to have anything go wrong with us."

I think I am right, Mother, and I can stand getting a little hurt if necessary. When I see him and he sees me, perhaps we shall not even connect and not love each other at all. At any rate I can find out what the score is and finish the business, if necessary. Do not worry. I think I am lucky to have even the hope of such a nice person, and it is a wonderful feeling to be loved by someone you fancy you love very much too.

All my love,
Marcia

P.S. I forgot to tell you about the palmist. She said a lot of true things about my personality and character. That Red Cross work was an interlude not connected with anything else in my life. That I need never worry about money. If I spend my last dollar, the next day something will come from the blue. Drama was very strong in my hand. She said who is J. Then she described Jim as he is, even to his face, pretty well. She told me something of his personality but said there is a mist around him. We correspond, she said, and he has a vital impression of me stamped on his mind and he loves me very much. She said I would marry this man or one like him. She said other things too. Funny thing is that just before I went to her I had written a letter to Jim telling him I appreciated and believed in his sincerity and that he should not worry about losing me or words to that effect.

Of course, I do not believe in fortune telling, but she was a little bit psychic and I was pleased.

Marcia Ward Behr

Beachhead Landings

The war news from the Pacific had been encouraging in January 1943, when I was applying to go overseas with the Red Cross. The six-month struggle for the island of Guadalcanal had ended and all Japanese resistance in Papua New Guinea had ceased. I thought about where the Red Cross might send me — China, India, North Africa, England — anywhere but New Guinea!

There was a lull in troop movements for the first few months after I arrived in Cairns, Australia, in May 1943. It must have been because fighting on two oceans created shortages of ships and aircraft carriers, especially in the Pacific. Beachhead landings on islands north of Guadalcanal were delayed. When the men did leave Cairns for combat, I never knew where they were going. Security was very tight. Of course, by March 1944, Red Cross women had been working in a few coastal bases of Papua New Guinea and Guadalcanal for almost a year.

By the end of my Sydney leave that March 1944, the Allies had been so successful in beachhead landings and seizures of the islands north of Guadalcanal, that they were able to cross the Bismarck Sea and take over the Admiralty Islands, including the superb, deep, landlocked harbor of Manus — a vital staging base where I eventually spent a night.

Lieutenant Jim Wilder, in charge of an LST (Landing Ship Tank), probably was attached to Rear Admiral Barbey's Amphibious Forces of the U.S. Navy. They operated out of Jim's base, Milne Bay at the eastern end of Papua New Guinea. The landing barges transported Allied troops and tanks onto enemy-held beachheads, often in the dark of night and under heavy enemy fire. Barbey's barges surely were involved in securing the Admiralties.

It was after the victory over the Japanese in the Admiralties (while I was on leave in Sydney) that I received a bunch of delayed letters from Jim, forwarded to me from Cairns. It had been a month since I last heard from him.

COFFEE and SYMPATHY
World War II Letters from the Southwest Pacific

[Sydney]
March 21, 1944

Dearest Family,

Well, my leave is almost up. I have rested as well as played a bit. I have not been a very good tourist but I have had enough glimpses to know what the city is like. I have had a date every night but two and, on one of those, Ann Lally and I went to a concert, so I have had a good time. Of course I have not been able to choose my escorts, but they have all been pleasant if not exciting. The one who was most attentive and sent me flowers went to the hospital soon afterwards with, possibly, jungle ulcers. I went to see him on Saturday afternoon and took him some carnations and roses. He seemed to appreciate my coming very much and Sunday night I saw a friend of his who also thanked me for going to see him. I shall go again if I can.

For heaven's sake, do not worry about my relationship to my friend Jim. I am sure it is right and good. As I piece together what I remember about him, he is really a fine person. I remember how sweet he was the night of the dance, and really gave those old people a wonderful time. He was with them most of the evening and saw that they got milk and cookies at intermission. He may have done it for me because he knew they came out to Yorkies to pass approval on the dance, but, at any rate, he did it. I remember the next morning, when Marge was sweeping the ballroom, he and another lieutenant grabbed brooms and would not let Marge do it. (Marge being the waitress.)

I have no idea about his family nor do I know anything very specific about his background, except where he went to college, his age, that he is separated from his wife and things I have already told you. I try to tell him about me and I write to him as I would to you, because I feel that he cannot possibly have learned to know me from the short time he was at Yorkies. Of course, he saw me under favorable circumstances. I looked well. I probably seemed very capable. It is a romantic setting and I was gay. His friends liked me too and you know, when you feel popular, you are at your best.

A strange thing happened last night. I had planned to stay in and write letters, not having a date anyhow. About 8:30 p.m. one of the girls came in and asked me if I wanted to go out. She said Alan, his name, was attractive so I accepted. When the three boys arrived, the other dates were nurses and the girl came back and said it is the wrong Alan but he was nice too. Having committed myself, I went. For goodness sake, it was an Air Corps boy who had stayed at Yorkies Knob for ten days last August. I was relieved and so was he. The nurses were not especially pretty. Alan and I had a fun talking over the old times at our rest home. He said, which I never knew, that the place had meant so much to him and that I had been so kind to him and his friend. He said he had had a crush on me. Well, I certainly never encouraged him. They happened to be about the only permanent guests at the time and I was nice to them, I am sure.

I have done some good and made a few people contented for a little while. Jim has written in his letters, when mine might have sounded discouraging to him, that I am doing a lot by just being here, that what they all want is a sweet American girl to see or talk to once in a while. I have tried to stay the way I was before. I am perhaps a little more sure of myself and it is easier for me to talk to just anybody.

I wonder where they will send me next. Perhaps right back to Sydney. Then I might have a chance of seeing Jim and some of the others. If it were not for that, I think I would feel I might just as well be home as in a big city over here.

. Love,
Marcia

[Sydney]
March 23, 1944

Dearest Family,

Well, what do you think? I am in love. It is fate, yes, that is it. If I had fallen before, I might have gotten married and never have come overseas and met Jim. I am so glad I wrote honestly and told him that I loved him and trusted him before his two letters came yesterday. In one of them he said he is about to become a single man again. He said, "For the gory details on my marital front and also to keep you in the light as far as I am concerned, so as to remove the vulture hue I have donned, is that I am on the verge of being a single man again. Rather a lousy procedure to go through but you have no idea just how much it means to me to assume such a role. Seems that both of us have learned the hard way that there must be much deliberation before marriage. I am so glad there was no mess involved as the reason for such a decision. That I do not go for! And another point being that the war had nothing to do with it since we decided before to do it."

He loves me, of that I am sure; whether he will when we meet again remains to be seen. I only know that I feel like the luckiest girl in the world because, from what I do remember of him and from what I know of him through his letters, he is a superb human being. He is very wise, mature and good, I am positive of that.

He writes so beautifully and easily and from the heart. He believes in speaking out and not holding back on issues. He really did make me fall in love with him. I just went with the tides and now I can hardly breathe without thinking about him.

I do not want him to think he cannot back out or that I expect too much of him. I hope he does not think I wrote only as soon as I heard that he was single. I would be the vulture then; that is what I told him, too. It is quite marvelous. I feel that I can tell him anything. I can talk about the flowers I see or the monkeys in the zoo or the house being fumigated or anything.

I did not know I actually loved him until a week ago last Tuesday. There was something about his letter and I prayed some and fought the doubts and won. I cannot say whether I would have loved him if he had never had a marriage mist around him. This produced anxiety in me and that made a conflict and it made me think and it came out in my letters, and his letters were stronger for all of that, I am sure. It produced a short cut to a real understanding of each other and the way our minds work.

All my love,
Marcia

Marcia Ward Behr

Brisbane

It was the first of May 1944, and I had just ended a great leave in Sydney and was headed 900 miles north to Brisbane where I had been assigned to the largest enlisted-men's club in the Pacific. Down under in the late fall the weather was perfect with flowers in full bloom in every park and garden.

Brisbane is a pleasant city with modern buildings, hotels, libraries, universities, and attractive houses perched on hills above the river banks. The wide, deep river winds through the heart of the city where ocean-going vessels dock, and downstream wharves are also within easy reach of the metropolis.

The population of Brisbane at the time of World War II was over 300,000 — a city big enough for the military to enjoy theaters, restaurants, ballrooms, outdoor sports and splendid nearby beaches.

Our Red Cross club could accommodate 300 men overnight and thousands of G.I.s on leave streamed into the club daily to benefit from its many services — meals, rooms, barbershop, library, day trips, dances, information and smiles from the staff. Maybe they just wanted a shoeshine or a watch repaired, or to borrow a hat because the M. P. would pick them up on the street without one, and they had lost theirs in a restaurant.

"I was supposed to meet a guy here in the lobby at 6 o'clock," a soldier would say to me. "Did you see him? He was short and dark. It's quarter after six and I have to go. Did you see him?" I looked over the room at the hundreds of boys milling around just standing and smoking, or looking up names in the register, or waiting in line for the canteen, or sitting and reading the paper. I said, "Leave a note for him and put it on the bulletin board." He wrote, "Harry, I had to go back to camp. See you Thurs. Same time, same place. Andy." I hoped that Harry would see the message.

Then Mike, a Marine, handed me a rose as I walked toward the recreation hall. He had talked to me for a long time when I first saw him. He had limped up to me unsteadily on crutches one day when I was fixing the bulletin board. He had been drinking a lot.

"You think I'm drunk, don't you, and maybe I shouldn't talk to you. I don't care." Yes, I said, "you have had something, I can see that, but that's all right, Mike." "You're very sweet," he said. He was so young and had such big brown eyes. We sat down at a checker table.

"Want to play?" I asked. We didn't play. He wanted to talk. He told me about the Red Cross girl who had taken care of him on the LST (Landing Ship Tank) which brought him back from New Britain where he had been wounded. He talked about his home in Chicago and his mother and father, and every once in a while he said, "I'm drunk, but you think I am all right, don't you?" "Yes, Mike, you're all right." I put some records on the loudspeaker and Mike limped away. About an hour later he came back and handed me an orchid corsage. It was beautiful. I used to see Mike once a week, and I never saw him drunk again. One day he said he was going back to the hospital for another operation on his leg. Soon after that I was transferred to New Guinea.

While I was very busy in this huge club, the Allies were moving closer to the battle for the Philippines. Brisbane was the headquarters of General Douglas MacArthur, the commander of the South Pacific Forces. He would eventually keep his promise and return to the Philippines to set free his American soldiers imprisoned there by the Japanese since the beginning of the war.

[Brisbane]
April 1, 1944

Dearest Family,

Much to my surprise Marjorie and I are both to be stationed at Brisbane. It is a huge club operation — probably the biggest club over here. Well, I wanted a change and this is certainly it. I am hoping to do a good job.

Being in a large club like this, one can easily see the need of the Red Cross. This place is very well organized and, as far as I can see, everyone likes each other and they are quite happy. The work is not hard but the hours are long and, for me the newness is a strain, and the numbers of people, the confusion and noise seem quite exhausting. Of course, each person who comes to you for attention comes with the same verve and you just have to return the same. Even when you just walk across the room, you must be ready to "give out." The boys do not understand anything else. Every minute you are watched by someone. Most of them think somewhat alike. They've been doing the same things and talking about the same things with each other for so long. Just like the rest of us, they are trying to hang on to some form of security and existence, even if they would not admit or realize it.

There is every service for the boys in this club — over three hundred beds, with pressing facilities and showers. The food is not bad at all. The snack bar is open day and night. Shoeshine, mending, library and record library. The library is the nicest spot. It is a quiet, large room with several windows and comfortable seats. There is plenty to read but the supply of magazines diminishes quickly. I like that duty.

The lobby is huge — a great help because of the numbers of boys who just mill through there not knowing which way to turn. Some of them strike out and find activities, others wait for something to drop on them. The information desk is always busy — questions, questions (about money, marriage licenses, eating places, what's in the club and where to get this or that). It is a very busy place. I shall be there tonight. Of course I do not know the answers, but there are files and others can help me. Bed-booking is in this lobby too and off to one side are the hospitality center and the program office.

They have established a theatrical department. I just do not understand what is wrong with me that I do not do more about getting into this work. The heads are away for the moment. I shall talk to them when they come back. The way the war is tooting along, everything is in a state of change. The Army moves out of here and there and the Red Cross follows them. Making reassignments is difficult now. This is a temporary assignment for me.

It is nearly six and I have had my dinner. Soon I go on duty at the information desk. It is Sat. night and the place is jammed and jumping. I only hope I can get through tonight and answer a few questions. Will write again.

All my love,
Marcia

[Yorkies Knob]
March 23, 1944

Marcia dear,

Received your telegram just now and with very mixed feelings digested the contents. Somehow or other I always felt you'd be back but, for your own peace of mind I'm glad, and hope you get something you like.

Yorkies has changed a lot. You would certainly be very unhappy around here. I don't like to put things in letters, but one of these days I'll tell you personally. Mrs. Hayhoe gave notice — then was asked to stay — then the next day was told off for making a noise in the kitchen, so promptly walked off. All the staff is unhappy. I don't blame them. They never get any praise, only picking on all day.

From the number of letters I repost, I should say Jim Wilder's emotions are getting the better of him. Must go now, Marcia. I hope you are feeling the benefit of your rest and that you are happy wherever you go.

Lots of love,
Marie

[Brisbane]
April 6, 1944

Dearest Family,

I shall enclose a letter I received from Marie today. I certainly got out of Yorkies just in time. I would be miserable there now — no position, no work and no guests. Whew!

I shall tell you "My Day." Yesterday, let me see, I went up the hill to the nurses' home for breakfast because I can always get an egg there. Then I took the tram (trolley) downtown and walked the block to the club. A few people (soldiers) always stand in the doorway, and I begin to loosen my lips for a ready grin in case it is needed. I try to prepare my eyes, too, so the smile won't be all teeth and no sparkle. I breezed into the program office, looked on the schedule and found I was on duty in the recreation room all day. First, I must get the bus off to a beach. Marjorie says it is a terrible place. At any rate, I went sweetly up to everyone to drum up trade. I managed to get two people who had planned to go anyway. The bus came at ten and we dismissed it because not enough people wanted to go. It seems foolish to have any trip like that if it is not popular. I hate to have to use high-pressure salesmanship.

Then I straightened the maps with the help of a boy I promised to play Ping-Pong with and then I played Ping-Pong. Meanwhile, every few minutes some queer little duck, who lives on our street in New York City, approaches me. He is always before me since he discovered our proximity. He wants me to play Ping-Pong. He wants me to dance. He wants me to have a cup of coffee with him, a Coca-Cola, some ice cream. He wants me to go to the movies with him. Please, will I dance with him at the dance? I have not been to a dance so far and I dread it a little — all they do is jitterbug. Then I fixed the flowers — goldenrod — in the rec hall and lobby. Then I went on an errand to get material for a war map and some candy to put in the Easter baskets. Then I had lunch, then went out to the railroad station to get the holiday changes in time tables. Then back to making more baskets. A few interested spectators made remarks and asked questions. At 6:30 my day was over. I ate supper at the club and came home about 7:30. I wrote a couple of urgent letters but did not feel like writing Jim. I shall write him later.

Do you mind my telling you about Jim? All remains to be seen, but I do not see how I could love anyone more and I am positive he is very sincere. We must pray for his safety. I think of him as surrounded by love and good and everything safe I can think of. I told him about my always wanting to be a good actress and he certainly was sweet about that. "You can and shall be a marvelous actress, and I, as a sort of cheering squad, am going to see to it that it comes to pass." It is nice that someone who has never seen me act has so much faith in me.

Well, I must get a good night's sleep. We have to be at work by 9 a.m.

Love,
Marcia

[Brisbane]
April 10, 1944

Dearest Family,

I received a wonderful letter from Tom. He suggested that I do some writing. I will next time I feel inspired, but right now there is nothing to give me a lift. Something will break through soon and I may feel the urge.

Naturally, the one thing I am most happy about is Jim Wilder. I certainly hope you are not worrying about me along this subject. I am positive that it is right. Something way down so very deep assures me.

A funny thing happened last night. We had an Easter review of little children for entertainment at the Red Cross Club. It was perfectly adorable and the tots ranged from two to ten. They were talented, wore excellent costumes and performed creatively under good direction. Well, I went over and stood in a corner to see the performance.

Naturally, I spoke to the soldier next to me. I asked him his state and he said he came from Hartford, Conn. He happened to know Jim Wilder very well as Jim had left Yale to coach basketball and teach history in a high school in Hartford. This boy said he used to go trout fishing with him. He raved about Jim and said he is a "smoothie." He said he left Hartford and went to Harvard. He said his father owns a large summer camp in Maine. I hope he is not too much of an athletic fiend. I am sure I would never have the strength to keep up with him. This boy said he was a star basketball player. Of course, I did not dare show too much enthusiasm and just patiently waited for him to tell me about Jim.

From Jim's latest letters I think he may be getting a leave quite soon. He has been up there in a pretty hot area for almost six months. He has been sick with dengue fever which is quite miserable and saps your strength for quite a time. It is from a mosquito bite and is a bit like measles and flu simultaneously.

Since Jim has had one experience in a hasty marriage, I know he will not be hasty again in anything. Of course, when he sees me, he may change his mind anyway. You can never tell about these things. I shan't be hurt, though, and what is right will happen and nothing else. I write him everything hoping he will not have any great illusions; after all up there away from it all he could exaggerate even upon his imagination. Don't worry, Syl, I much prefer to come home and be married, if and when. I do not know, maybe I am crazy. Perhaps he made me fall in love with him or perhaps I am just romantic. I have seen a lot of men, though, and being an American and attractive, I could have acquired at least one or two aspirants, but no one affected me so I went on in my own sweet way.

Actually, when I first saw Jim, even though he was fun, I was not touched by him one way or another. I thought he was very good looking, clean-cut, well-bred and decent. Perhaps, because I knew he was a married man and I only saw him for such a short time, I was not affected by him, but I certainly like him now and can scarcely wait to see him again. Tomorrow I am going down to the beach. It is about 50 miles from Brisbane and I have been by train before. I hope to see Ann Lally who is stationed at an officers' rest home there. We saw each other in Sydney while we were both on leave. It is nice to have this ocean spot to visit on days off.

It is so wonderful for you and Daddy to be free from lack. I am so happy for you all.

Love,
Marcia

[Brisbane]
April 13, 1944

Dearest Family,

Actually, last night was my first G.I. dance here in this huge club. The orchestra was a bit sad, very small and Aussie. That cast a pathetic note on the dance from the start. I compared my feelings to the U.S.O. dance I went to in New York. I was so scared there — strange men in uniform. Each one I talked to was either a farmer or a truck driver. They were shy, too, and I was most uncomfortable. Last night, in my uniform, I just stood on the steps and compared — they were all Americans in uniform and strangers because this is a club for many, many transient servicemen — going to or coming from the war zone. I felt no shyness and was not a bit self-conscious standing there. Whether anybody wanted to dance with me or not, it did not matter. Besides, 10 percent of the men get out on the floor with a twisted, determined look and jitterbug, and 90 percent stand on the sidelines and gawk and would not dance for love or money. Then a smiling little sailor asked me to dance. He jittered and I did something. He did say that I could make a good Stateside jitterbugger.

Sally Howe, the program director, introduced me to Larry Ross, an old-time veteran of vaudeville and night clubs. He is nearly forty, although he looks younger. He talked my ears off and my eyes out. I only said enough to show my interest in the stage. He was interesting but exhausting because he allowed no time for responses. He does not listen. He has imagination and has written lots of hit songs and plays, but I do not see how he could ever be an artistic actor because an actor must listen or how can his speeches ever ring true?

This morning Sally Howe asked me if I would perform for the variety show we are planning. I should do it whether I am a flop or not.

It is three days since I have heard from Jim. I should be patient but I want to hear that he is over the dengue fever and I wonder if my letters accepting his love will scare him. I doubt it but it is amusing to muse.

                                                                              Love,
                                                                             Marcia

---

[Brisbane]
April 18, 1944

Dearest Family,

This morning I have been practicing my scenes for the amateur show on Thursday night. I am going to come out and explain to the audience how every actress has to give auditions and what an ordeal it is — dark theatre, empty stage, one man in the audience upon whom your very life and career seem to hang.

Then I shall do three monologues: Granny Sparks, Sonya from *Uncle Vanya,*, and Topsy. They can't be too terrible and at least they have variety.

I had a wonderful day at the beach yesterday. George Flowers, an old friend from Cairns, was there. He reminded me of all the many friends who think a lot of me. He told me that any number of people are interested in my welfare. I told him about Jim and, since they are both in the same territory, George said he will look him up and see if he is good enough for me. Very complimentary, isn't it? George also said that I must remember to always make the man I love believe he is the most wonderful person in the world, that men are egotistical above all things.

When I got home I went to the club and found a lot of mail. There were letters from you and two letters from Jim. He did understand and followed all my thinking in accepting his love for me. Sometimes it is a bit up in the clouds or at least searching. I feel certain now that he does love me. He is good, I am sure of it and I only hope and pray that he does not have illusions about me. I try to improve my disposition daily and to keep my eyes open and be alert to observe and learn. He must remember what I look like. People are always telling me or thinking that I am pretty, but I know what I look like. I do not want people to get unreal ideas. He knows I read the Bible and he says he is reading it every day too.

I feel sure I know Jim because, when I write, he understands. In fact, he answers things before I ask them and vice versa. Perhaps it is all crazy but it seems to be the thing I have always wanted. He says again: "I am sure that your interests concerning the stage will be something for both of us to have."

Jim says "something is up" and he cannot get leave for some time probably. It is a bit hard but I try not to feel any separation and what is to be will be. I am anxious to know what you think about all this, but I am sure you are with me.

Love,
Marcia

[Brisbane]
April 24, 1944

Dearest Family,

    The day of the act finally came. Marjorie was in charge of getting the acts together and she had collected a lot of mighty good, mostly musical, talent. The only worry was the M.C. (not her doing), but he had been asked, so she had to use him.

I wore a white cotton dress and low heels. I waited backstage for my turn. I heard the audience and knew I was in for the worst. They were heckling. They did not like the M.C. from the start. The various acts, when they got under way, were applauded and liked, but they certainly were not prepared for anything like me. In the first place, I didn't use a mike because I needed to move around. The street noises can be heard inside the auditorium and the acoustics are bad anyway. There are large pillars everywhere. The M.C. announced me and out I went onto the stage. I was the only acting piece on the program. I do not think many people heard my introduction. I didn't even finish it and went right into Granny. That they heard because they were still, but they did not understand what was happening. It was so out of the blue, so unlike anything vaguely familiar to most of them that they were dumbfounded. However, my energies were aroused and I was determined. I finished and there were murmurs and some applause. The M.C. said, "Don't you want Marcia to do another?" They acquiesced and, so I plunged into Topsy and then Sonya and then literally stooped over and crawled off the stage.

Whether they applauded or not, I do not know. The M.C. said I should have come out when he called for a bow. I did not hear him. Funny thing is, I knew it was a good acting job and that the experience was invaluable. I had forced myself to do something that was almost impossible. Before I went on stage a Navy man, an old stock trouper who played a "mean" guitar and sang, spoke to me and said, "Baby, I would not be in your shoes for anything. That takes nerve. You have your hands full." Afterwards he congratulated me and I knew he liked the act. He told others as much. The next day a few people raved about my work. When I came off stage, I was not frantically upset. I shook a bit from the nervous strain. When I was alone I laughed at myself and I literally admired myself for my nerve.

The war news is so good. I wonder if Jim is in action. I am trying to think constructively about his safety. What use depression? In his last letter Jim said he is trying not to think of the mileage which separates us but concentrating on the proximity of our thoughts. That is the real thing anyway and that tie is strong and the only lasting one. I miss you all so much and, as the second year overseas comes up, I wonder how soon I shall see you again.

I may get into the theatrical stuff very soon, but all good things come to him, her, who waits. Pollyanna!

All love,
Marcia

COFFEE and SYMPATHY
World War II Letters from the Southwest Pacific

[Brisbane]
end of April, 1944

Dearest Family,

    I received lots of letters from you today including one from Sylvia and the clippings about the theatre and yours, Mother, about the concert and the round-table discussion of my love life. Naturally, you are all very curious but, relax, everything has to come out in the wash. I have not heard from Jim in five days but he has been writing every day when he can. For all I know he may be very busy now because there is certainly a lot going on in the Pacific, as you can see by the papers.
    About Jim's family, I know nothing. Whether he has money, I know not nor do I care. He is intelligent and capable enough to get along in the world. He has had advantages and a college education, I know that. In fact, I am quite positive that you would like him. He is attractive looking, there is no denying that and he is youthful, though thirty years of age. In fact I am not a bit sorry he has been married before, he has grown up enough now to know what he wants. He has been persistent but I think he must have known within himself all along that it was the right thing for both of us. However, if it does not work out, cela m'est égal. It does not affect anyone but me and I am a big girl now and can conquer a lost personal cause.
    You are sweet to be so interested and I knew you would be. I told you because it is important to me and always before you have followed and shared my interests. Please do not worry about me. As a matter of fact, I have suddenly regained my enthusiasm for the theater and all life in general. I am not unhappy in my work, except that too many people ask you for your spare time and it is a strain making up excuses. I have talked to a lot of very interesting men and made some good friends here. I feel definitely more at home in my work. I do what I am told and try to be pleasant all the time. Statistics from a sailor, observing the Red Cross girls at the information desk, show we smile 133 times and answer 31 questions every five minutes. No wonder we get tired.
    I am now in the library making out cards for a new checking system. It is my idea so I guess it is up to me to do the work. I have been here since nine — at lunch I broke away to entertain a birthday party of four soldiers — and I think we had a good time — then back here until six-thirty.
    I am going to dinner tonight with a very nice sailor who has a home somewhere near Philadelphia. He was so persistent and seemed intelligent and a gentleman that I accepted. He knows that I am not interested in him so, if he

Marcia Ward Behr

wants to take me out on that basis and it gives him pleasure, well, that is all right. I had lunch yesterday with an amazingly brilliant young soldier. He has traveled all over — speaks many tongues and has read volumes for his age. You meet all kinds but it is tiring sometimes. Jim tells me to keep rested, that he "wants something to tear down to Aussie land to."

All my love,
Marcia

[Brisbane]
May 2, 1944

Dearest Mother and family,

    These are strange times and anything can happen. Have faith in me, though, because I am trying to do the right thing. I think I mentioned a sailor, Frank Jones is his name. This is my one-year anniversary in Australia and, after all this time, I am suddenly in a situation. It is all honest and straightforward and the right path must and shall be followed.

    About a week ago this same Frank Jones approached the information desk. He asked me some questions — I don't remember now. In a short time I gathered that he was educated and a gentleman and even had some interest in the theatre. He has blond reddish hair and even features, straight blue eyes, not beautiful. He is just a little taller than I am. He graduated from Bucknell in 1938. He is single. He asked me to have dinner with him at the club. I rather hesitated but he wanted me to very much and I thought it was a good idea to have dinner in the boys' dining room once in a while. He certainly seemed nice enough. So I did. He told me he expected to be here for some time and it would make him most happy if I would let him see something of me and take me out some. I certainly was not anxious to give in to him and finally told him that I was very much in love. Undaunted, he said he would still like to take me out one evening. I don't know why but I accepted an invitation to go to dinner and dancing at a night club in town where the drinks are no stronger than sarsaparilla. I was quite tired and did not talk much. Finally, Frank asked me to do some of the talking. I could not for the life of me think of one thing to say. He waited, then leaned back in his chair and said, "All right, I can amuse myself." And we just sat. He is really funny and I laughed and said that in self-defense I would have to say something.

    There was an A.R.C. party for one of the girls who is leaving for New Guinea. I had gotten tied up for the evening with an Air Corps captain whom I knew in Cairns. I really did not want to take him to the party and I knew that Frank was acquainted with some of the people invited and especially he knew the guest of honor, so I thought I would ask Frank to escort me, because I felt sure he would have a good time and add to the fun. I told the captain that I had to go to the party and would try to see him Tuesday night. He is a young married man from New York — progressively educated and he thinks I am intelligent — Bennington and all that. I took Frank to the party. We had fun and then, on the way home, he said he was desperately in love with me and wanted me to marry him. He knows that I love Jim but he is putting up an awful fight.

I came home and wrote a letter to Jim and told him that this person exists but that I want to love Jim. It was a long, long letter. Then, instead of mailing it, I gave it to Frank to read. It was his birthday and I had promised to have dinner with him. He read it and said, "Well, that's that. You love him and do not want to see me anymore." Then we just sat. We were in a very crowded lobby waiting for our turn to eat at one of the better but old-fashioned hotels. I was determined that was the way I wanted it. "Is that it?" he asked. "Yes," I said. He said, "Dammit, you like me, I know you do. You underestimate me," he said. "I am going to fight. You send this letter, only we will revise it a bit." He seemed very frank and sincere. I saw Frank again the next night and told him that all day I had been thinking about the situation and that I preferred to take the risk of losing him and waiting for Jim. I said I may end up as an old maid, but I would rather have it this way. He said he would have to be dead to have that happen. He said he had written home about me. He really has a lot of nerve. Then he said he had sent a letter to Jim himself asking him for his honest intentions concerning me. He said it was only fair to everyone to know the truth. So, you see, I am being tossed about. Frank never gets discouraged, he says, "You'll see, I grow on people."

I tell Frank it is not fair to Jim. He says he had his chance. It's true he did not tell me then how he felt. Of course he had less time. I keep asking Frank why he thinks he likes me. That makes him mad. He says I have so much character in my face. So, you see, Mother, someone else sees it too.

His manners are perfect except the way he uses his knife and fork, but that is probably three years of the Navy. He has been wounded three times and has all kinds of medals and distinctions. He is an engineer by profession. His favorite pastime is horseback riding. I am mailing my letter to Jim today. I do wish he were here because, although I do not love Frank, I am happy with him. There is no doubt about that and conversation is easy with him. Suddenly he gets so very serious and then I like him best. He made a bracelet for me, brought me some fruit and a bottle of olives. It is nice for one's ego.

As I said before, there are so many people here. No life of our own of any kind. I have not changed. I try to be sincere and aboveboard in everything and that is all I can do.

Marcia Ward Behr

You said once not to close my mind to other people and I haven't. Now you have my emotional status up to date. I shall keep you informed.

All my love,
Marcia

[Brisbane]
May 10, 1944

Dearest Family,

    I know I have not written in some time but I just did not know what to say. My mind must have been slipping to write that letter to Jim. You told me to keep an open mind about heart interests and I did. Now I regret the whole Frank interlude. I really do not like him at all. Maybe I am being unfair to the boy but there is just something about him that I do not like nor that I can trust. Perhaps it is the fact that he wrote that letter to Jim and then a few days later said he did not send it, when he specifically told me he had mailed it. He had a nerve to write it in the first place. Now it is embarrassing to have been so honest in writing to Jim. However, if Jim does not understand it all as I explained it to him and wants to let everything drop, then I guess the whole thing has been a beautiful dream. Somehow or other he will understand but I am preparing myself, or trying to, for the worst.

    I wish sometimes that I were not so naive. For the past week I have been in a terrible state and about my work too. It is dull and I feel useless. I was just marking time before taking some definite steps, either for a transfer or to come home. I do get darn lonely. Everyone does over here. If you are working hard you forget, but I have had a lot of time to think lately.

    Tonight my hopes soared a bit. They do need me in the theatrical dept. They need someone to play certain parts. By chance, I sat next to the assistant director tonight and he asked me if I had had any theatrical experience. I told him and he was very interested. Club directors are loath to lose any of their staff but if there is a specific part for someone and they cannot find an actress, I told him I am the girl. So you see perhaps all good things do come to those who wait.

All my love,
Marcia

COFFEE and SYMPATHY
World War II Letters from the Southwest Pacific

[Brisbane]
May 18, 1944

Dearest Family,

I received a letter today from my dear friend, Mrs. Hayhoe — jolly, fat, philosophical, backbone of Yorkies Knob. It was so simple and typical of her. She says everyone is unhappy at Yorkies. The staff only stays because of good wages and rumors that the place will soon close. Liquor appears and is consumed even at the tables now. (We never allowed it about the place.) The staff's children are not allowed to be seen. Of course Arlene and I spoiled the staff, but they were part of the place and the guests wandered freely into the kitchen and it was a home. I sent Mrs. Hayhoe's letter on to Jim because he will remember her and he will also see that, fortunately for me, I got out of there in good time.

Now I must tell you of my great joy. I have received all my Christmas packages, They are just as welcome in May as December. Thank you all.

I have not heard from Jim in over ten days. He may have moved farther on. I somehow feel that he will understand that incident. It certainly proved to me that I really and truly love Jim. There is no doubt in my mind now. Still, do not worry about me.

Frank Jones may come and see you in New York. I had not seen him for a couple of weeks. He came in and asked me to go to dinner, said he was leaving soon. I accepted for dinner, but he left before the dinner date. I gave him your address, so I am pretty sure he will call when or if he comes to N. Y.

I had some souvenirs made for my sisters (Muffy now being in the family) and shall send them to you. They are the best things I can find. I shall keep looking for the rest of you. Enclosed is a letter you may enjoy from my dear friend Rex Shawl. You remember Joe Flynn spoke about my being funny, well, this is the man who was there at Yorkies and made me funny. You can get a vague idea from this letter. Also, you may recall we went to a lovely falls and rode horseback.

                                          Love,
                                          Marcia

Marcia Ward Behr

New Britain
May 3, 1944

Dear Marcia,

    Three more long months have rolled by since I last wrote you and because of your promptness in answering my last letter I thought I would try it again and hope that you will answer this one. As you can see by the heading we are still where we were three months ago and everything is quiet now, practically to the boring stage. It is a lazy life and I should revel in it but because of some perverse streak in my makeup I am strangely discontent. We are going back to join the regiment soon and perhaps that will help. What I think I need is a little time at Yorkies Knob where there was never a dull moment, at least while I was there.
    We have heard rumors, unconfirmed of course, that Arlene has returned Stateside and that all is quiet and peaceful at Yorkies. I don't know whether this is true or not, Rosebud, but if you would care to tell me, I'd like to know. How about your leave — have you had it yet and did you have a good time? If so, let your lil brother know all about it. I'll wager that by this time you are thoroughly fed up with Australia and would like to be back in the States again.
    Your last letter caused a sensation here and I thought you'd be interested in hearing about it. We have a lieutenant here of obvious Irish descent who has always been the butt of all our ribbing. He is rather dumb and extremely gullible. One night, after the arrival of your letter, Ernie Smith, the lieutenant and I were sitting in the tent alone and just talking and Ernie winked at me and remarked about how it rained the night we played Moline, Illinois. I took him up on it and we batted the breeze about how we had played vaudeville. I remarked about our feminine partner, Rosebud, and Ernie, who was at the Knob the night we made our debut, if you will remember — Rosebud and Stinker [see letter, Oct. 27, 1943], took it up. Kirkpatrick scoffed at the idea of our being on the stage and we just ignored him. Our imaginations ran riot and we really had a time. Ernie described me and him in sailor straw hats, with strings attached to our lapels, blue and white blazers, white flannel trousers and tan shoes coming dancing out on the stage and singing, "No! No! A Thousand Times No!" I, not to be outdone, essayed a little soft-shoe routine, the only one I know and we got a boot out of it and Kirk was goggle-eyed. We went to great lengths to describe the beauteous Rosebud who in tights, bangles and black silk hose added so much to our act. I threw out the bait by telling Ernie that I had received a letter from her recently and Kirk said he didn't believe it. I told him it was okay, to forget it, but he was nearly consumed with curiosity and called us liars etc. Finally, I said that he had asked for it and I got your letter and showed him the first paragraph. As you will recall you mentioned that your script was bad and you thought of taking up tight-

wire walking because it gave you poise. You even called me Stinker. Kirk read it and was almost satisfied but one thing stuck in his mind. How about Ernie Smith? I flipped over to the last paragraph and there you had asked me to give your regards to all, especially Ernie Smith. That's all he needed and to this day he'll scream at anyone who dares say that "Smith, Rosebud and Shawl" (my concession to age and beauty in the billing) were not in vaudeville. Since that time he has always asked us about the theatre and does he get it! It taxes our imagination at times but his enthrallment at our thespian escapades is worth it. He always goes around quoting Ernie's remark about the thing that caused vaudeville's demise. "Radio will not last." I thought you'd be interested in this and if you write again and pray God you do just make some crack about the old team and I assure you it will be put to good use.

I hope this finds you well, Rosebud, as it does me and happy too. We think of you and often. Poor kid, exposed to all of those Navy men. You letters are gratefully accepted and are much welcomed. If Marie is there still extend to her my regards. Write if you can, please.

As ever,
Rex

[Brisbane]
May 22, 1944

Dearest Family,

My goodness, but my Jim is more wonderful than I had thought. After two weeks of mental "hell" for me I received a letter from him. Apparently there is one before this that I have not received. He is such a big person and so understanding and he really does love me as I love him, of that I am so very sure. Most marvelous news — he is taking leave. Whether I am hurrying it along, I do not know, but he must need one badly after nearly eight months near the firing line. I am so excited that I am subnormally calm.

Too bad you sent the perfume. I shall be wallowing in sweet scent. Well, I shall save it and bring it home with me, when I return. There is certainly no if about it. Lord knows when, though. I would certainly like to be home by Christmas, but I do not want to leave if there is a chance of seeing Jim. He said in his letter, "I want to convince an American Red Cross gal that it was worth waiting seven months for. You have been marvelous, Marcia. There are not many girls as alone as you are, that would have been as fine as you. You did not know me too well and yet you were willing to bank on me and our future. I need you and I need that security just as much as you need what, perhaps, I can give you. I don't care what outward appearance we put up; it's known that all of us over here are just plain tired out and on nervous tension. We know that nothing can or ever will lick us but nevertheless if I, for example, did not have these operations to look forward to, I would die of boredom and just quit." It's easier to quote from his letter and then you get more of an insight.

I believe Nan graduates today and it is so wonderful. I wish I were there and could have heard her speech. She is such a fine, stable person. I wish I had some of her balance and maturity. I shall probably never grow up in lots of ways. Gee, I miss you all. Everything sounds great at home.

Love,
Marcia

[Brisbane]
June 11, 1944

My Dearest Family,

Jim sent me his picture today. I wish you could see it and understand how good and clean and sweet he is. Did I ever tell you what he does look like? He is tall, well-built, being an athlete. He has bright blue eyes, brown straight hair, a beautifully shaped head, a large mouth, a long face, even teeth and a straight nose. His whole face lights up when he smiles and at other times he looks thoughtful. His vocabulary is extensive and I know he reads a lot. He loves me and that is wonderful.

The work is routine and I had not heard from Jim in a while. Sometimes I get a bunch together and sometimes only one. I try to write most every day because I started the habit when I was on leave in Sydney. Some of my letters are drab but if I long for letters here, he must doubly look for them up there. He rarely fails to mention the fact that my letters mean everything to him, I know one thing: He knows plenty about me from my writing. I know him because of the way he accepts my thoughts. It must be very hard for him to find anything to write about where he is.

You gave me a big hint in your last letter about Tom and Muffy! It is too marvelous! You and Daddy going to be grandparents, Tom and Muffy — mother and father, and the rest of us aunts. I shall buy some of the good, cheap wool here and send some home for you and Nan to knit and then I shall attempt some tiny garments myself.

I shall try to write more often.

All my love,
Marcia

[Brisbane]
June 13, 1944

Dearest Family,

It is a rainy, cold, nasty night and I am home in my room. Claudia, my roommate, is still at work. Perhaps I did not tell you that we are in the Yale apartments, the best place in town to live. After Marjorie left and went to an assignment in a far southern city, I had to endure transient roommates coming and going at all hours, a different girl every night. I know of a single room soon to be empty and I have gone through the right Army channels this time to get it.

Claudia Twiggs, my present mate, is from Atlanta, Georgia, very nice, quiet and agreeable. She has a radio and also a friend who brings her eggs that we just never see around here. Naturally I share in both of these luxuries. We take our eggs down to the club every morning and they fix them for us. I wonder if you get any of the same?

About the theatre deal — the whole thing fell through. Nothing to it. All those people out of work and seeking other jobs. So that is that.

I do not want to go to New Guinea. Not one man has ever advocated it. I should think girls would be an annoyance rather than much help in that abnormal place. I am not afraid of living conditions or diseases but the abnormalities — so many men and the few women can hardly scratch the surface. If I stay, I would rather hang on back here until we can make a jump beyond New Guinea. Besides, I imagine that place is a base section now and pretty much behind the lines. I really do not think "one has not lived if he has not experienced New Guinea." I can get along without it.

Jim's last letter spoke about his wrist in a cast, perhaps that is why his letters are few and far between. I hope it is not a bad accident. His letter was short and his handwriting very shaky. He said it was nothing bad.

I think you know everything and then probably I have just written it to Jim.

Love,
Marcia

Marcia Ward Behr

[Brisbane]
June 18, 1944

Dearest Family,

Milton Reick, the director of the theatricals in our club, asked me if I would step in and do a part in the last play, *The Women*. If Jim comes in the midst of it, I won't see much of him. This is a certainty, also they need me and I am here to do a job and this is part of it. I have no idea when Jim is coming. It is an obvious opportunity. There is only one other A.R.C. girl in the cast and the rest are Aussies. It is an all-women cast. Clare Boothe wrote it. It is not a big role but something like the character of Judith in *Stage Door*. The part has good, witty lines. It opens Friday — four days of rehearsal, but I know my lines. In my room tonight I was doing a good job — now if I can bring that to rehearsal and performance, you would be proud to see me, I know.

My green dress is perfect, and I shall wear the tan plaid suit and perhaps put on Nan's grey coat instead of hunting up another suit for the next scene. I need a hat. The hats here are terrible, but, my part being comic one, it won't be a tragedy if I'm not a beauty queen.

Wish me luck. I shall let you know the results.

All my love,
Marcia

[Brisbane]
June 20, 1944

Dearest Family,

The latest — Jim was hit by an Army truck! "So I am now in the hospital with various and sundry injuries. All this happened a week ago and today is the first day I have been able to sit up and get a letter off to you." I cannot imagine whether it is very bad or not or what really happened to him. It was a relief to hear from him but a blow to find out why I had not heard. One thing, he has been getting lots of letters from me and perhaps that helps his spirits. He is still coming down on leave but I have no idea when. In a way I hope it is not until the end of July, because I shall be in *The Women* up to that time.

Our first performance is this Friday at a large Navy hospital and then we shall play the other hospitals and open in town here in a week or so. I will have about three rehearsals altogether but I am not worried. I shall be fairly good and get much better as we perform the play.

There is a bit of excitement around the club because one of the A.R.C. girls, who has been here a long time, is getting married on Saturday. She is even wearing a bride's white dress and we shall all be present. Then, afterwards there is a dinner at one of the big hotels. It is a good match and a safe and sane one, for they are fine people.

Yesterday a sailor, very young and natural, came up to the library desk. He started talking, asked me where I am from. I told him and he was confused. He thought I was an Aussie! He has been up north fifteen months and is down on leave. He wanted to talk and he did for about two hours! He talked about everything but especially about his part in the war — not naval secrets, of course, but really quite shocking and horrible things. I said, "Is it wise to go over it all with me?" And he said, "I think about it all the time so I may as well talk about it." Then, the inevitable of course: He wanted a date with an American girl. He was lonely and awfully tired and shaky, kind of holding himself together.

Claudia, my roommate, came along. She is a nice girl — sane, normal, understanding, natural, grows on you, certainly not especially pretty but darn nice. She wanted me to go have dinner with her. I knew I had to go to rehearsal afterwards, and then I just turned to the sailor and suggested he come along with us. Gosh, he was happy about it! However, we decided it was too late then. Claudia had to be back at 6:30, and all the restaurants were crowded, so we told the boy we would do it tonight and start earlier.

I saw him first thing this morning and he mentioned the dinner. At noon he said he was going horseback riding but would be back at 4:30. He appeared at 4:45 all ready to go! He and Claudia went ahead of me to get a table because I had to work until 5:30. We went to the Shingle Inn where they have quite tasty food. He talked and talked. He is about twenty, a farmer from Washington State. He told us about his girl, who has not written him, and he thinks she is letting him down but he is getting over that. He talked about his mother and father, aunts and uncles. He talked about skiing — he has won cups for this. He just bubbled. He was so happy. He said, up north, he sometimes smoked three packs of cigarettes a day. He said when he stops smoking he shakes and he was shaking from the cold weather down here anyway.

I think Claudia and I were both very happy too. I know I was. We laughed with him and enjoyed his good time so much. He asked to walk me home and then he said, "And let's walk Claudia to the Red Cross Club, so that the boys will see me with two American girls." He is going to Sydney on leave and I do hope he has a wonderful time! There are so many boys who need someone to listen to them. It would be marvelous if we could spread ourselves out and do things like that more often. It is at such moments that I feel most useful over here.

When you receive this letter I shall have performed quite a few times but wish me luck anyway.

All my love,
Marcia

[Brisbane]
June 24, 1944

Dearest Mama, Papa and Kids,

First, Mama dear, thank you so much for all the packages. My goodness, I have never had a better Christmas in all my life! [Still more presents had come.] Two days ago the Coty stuff arrived, so good and feminine. Simply divine! Then yesterday the marvelous blue Brooks sweater and the new purse, soap and the most beautiful nightgown and two of the nicest blouses, yum, yum, thanks! It was all worth waiting for six months.

Did I tell you that Trudy Johnson, A.R.C. and an old-standing member of this club, is to be married this afternoon — the first from this club — and it is going to be a perfect wedding? Mrs. Swope, the assistant club director and a marvelous person, is really doing a wonderful job preparing for it. Trudy is a lovely girl. She is marrying a boy she met at O.C.S. here. He is an officer now and is soon due to go back north again. He is in the infantry and has been overseas a long time. Both come from Michigan. We are all very happy about their happiness. The club personnel is giving her a silver tea service.

Last Thursday night ten of us who all live at Yale planned a shower for Trudy after 11 p.m. when everyone was through at the club. We asked her to come down to one of our rooms for a farewell get-together. Then, when everyone had gathered, we carried in a wastebasket sweetly decorated with pink crepe paper and chock-full of presents, topped with a corsage of white camellias. We were all so joyous. It was a shower just like home. Trudy was bowled over and very surprised and pleased. We had found pretty paper and ribbon donated by a frugal hoarder and everyone had been unselfish in giving away their treasured non-procurables. First she opened a box with a mother-of-pearl salt spoon and a butter knife and sugar spoon and some pink silk panties with elastic (just received from months of waiting)! Then she was given five beautiful white linen handkerchiefs. I gave her the Coty perfume received that very day. There was some nice bath powder and most amazing to all of us, two pairs of stockings! Two bridge luncheon sets and, let's see, a box of valuables (bobby pins, Mary Chess soap, lipstick, hand lotion), a darling little tropical painting done by one of the soldiers which Bobby Bredin gave her. Bobby is to be the only attendant. Then, after all, I remembered the white lace bra you sent me. I have not worn it yet and Trudy was delighted We had cheese and peanut butter and crackers, ripe olives and hot water and whisky. It was very cold — below freezing and no heat in the house.

They just decided to be married a week ago. A bride's dress is being made of distressed cargo material, a veil and shoes being borrowed. Last I heard, the groom still did not have his permission but we cannot be kept waiting at the church because another wedding is scheduled right afterwards. Ma Swope is planning the reception to be given at a nice hotel right across from the club.

I got so excited about the Christmas spirit yesterday that I suddenly decided to send home a box to all of you. It is not much and will probably savor of Aunt Lizzie, but it is the best I can do now. You have sent me so much and I want to send you something. I am sending Nan, Sylvia and Muffy each a bracelet handmade by U.S. soldiers out of Aussie money. Daddy's and Tom's presents are of Australian leather. Do not save your present, Mother, use it. Then I have enclosed odds and ends, pamphlets you can read, scan or toss out, feathered flowers made by the aborigines near Cairns, also the red beads. The coral necklace comes from Green Island off Cairns. Mrs. Hayhoe gave me the napkin ring and the matchbox case was given to me last Christmas by the Yorkies Knob staff. I sent them this morning so you may get them in a month or so.

Must stop, I am tired of writing and quite hungry. It is lunch time and I am in the club writing. Oh, the play — we gave it at a huge Army hospital last night. The audience liked it. I was good and got laughs.

Love,
Marcia

Marcia Ward Behr

[Brisbane]
July 2, 1944

Dearest Family,

I am now at the last rehearsal before we "open" here in town. Leta, the other A.R.C. girl in the play, and I broke into print again today — in the scandal sheet.

Yesterday I received a letter from an awfully nice officer who used to come with about ten other men every night to Yorkies Knob for dinner. We called them the "Odd Fellows" because the first time they came they went right upstairs to the veranda after dinner and smoked cigars and read and spoke to nobody. They thought it was only a convalescent home and one should speak in whispers and tiptoe. They were all attractive. He refers to the pancakes we tried to make with regular flour and no baking powder. We could not decide which was which in all the cans and used cream of tartar. The pancakes lay as flat in the pan as if they were just poured out and only became more like leather as they cooked. But it was fun.

Charlie Townes, an A.R.C. girl from our club, asked me to go out on a double date with some friends of hers. It turned out to be quite pleasant. They were young colonels. Mine was a head shorter, married and father of two young children and a gentleman, but then Charlie would only know nice people. We had a good steak dinner, then went to the vaudeville, the only "live" theater in town — pretty bad — like a long-drawn-out 1928 vaudeville in a small town, all kinds of acts and a chorus of dancing girls. Then we went to the house where one of them is billeted with other officers. We lit a fire in the fireplace — most houses here do not have such things — and then we scrambled some eggs. Such a treat! For a while at the club we never had any and, after eating all I wanted at Yorkies, it was a comedown. Now we get one or two a week, so things are looking up!

The wedding was lovely. There were numerous soldiers and sailors there and they practically whistled as the bride came down the aisle. The reception was held in a room at a hotel nearby. Only about 40 people were invited. There was a punch, sandwiches and the cake. We all chipped in for the cost which came to about $50 altogether. Can you imagine doing it for that price at home? Very cheap, n'est-ce pas?

I have not heard from Jim in about a week. I do hope he is all right. He did not say too much about his injuries so I am kind of in the dark about it all.

Just saw Hilda Thompson (former head of the Red Cross in Cairns) and she says I have a lovely family. So glad she came to see you. You should see some of the pretty flowers around now. Beautiful bright poppies. My room is full of them. I always try to keep flowers in the room.

All my love,
Marcia

COFFEE and SYMPATHY
World War II Letters from the Southwest Pacific

Miss Marcia Ward
c/o American Red Cross
APO 704

Lt. J.B. Bryan, Co. A.
542 Regt. APO 322
San Francisco
June 11, 1944

My dear Marcia —

Am enclosing a clipping which my wife sent to me recently. You should find it quite interesting.

I wonder if you still remember our gang. We are the ones who tacked the name of "shark-net Annie" to Arlene or whatever her name was. "We" were Fawlkes, Shuford, Backer, Whittier and Bryan, with a couple of others thrown in once in a while.

We still talk of the good times we had then, especially the Saturday evenings and the wonderful Sunday morning breakfasts.

Do you remember the Saturday night we tried to make pancakes and we used cream of tartar?

Here is another clipping you may find interesting. I think you used to know the officers.

Good luck.

Sincerely,
Johnny

[Brisbane]
July 5, 1944

Dearest Family,

Did I tell you that the club had planned a few weeks ago to have a county fair because they had one last year? One girl was to be in charge of a booth or an activity — shooting range, weight-guessing, chocolate wheel, lemonade and popcorn, fortune telling, dancing lessons by Mme. Mopanga, various slot machines with no money involved.

I was given the sideshow because at the first meeting I quite curiously asked who was going to take it and the director said, "You do it." Two other girls were in it with me. We met and discussed what we would do and that was as far as we got. Also we were asked to plan an act to wind up the ceremony. Implausible! We just did not know where to begin because in this club of transients you can hardly get you hands on anybody to make an appearance when you need them. Milton Reick, the theatrical director, was supposed to be approached to help us, but he was busy with the production of *The Women* to open in town the night before the fair. So we did nothing and ceased worrying about it. I went to Milton the day before and told him the freaks we had planned and that we would all be in it. Leta, who is a wonderful actress and is in the play with me, became the fat lady. She is really quite big. Another girl the bearded lady, and one the snake charmer and I the tallest lady in the world. I knew somehow the acts would go and Milton would help us. He did supply a four-year-old boy and a five-year-old girl for the midgets. They are really adorable child performers and dance and sing. Milton also arranged for the costumes.

Tuesday morning of the Fourth we started arranging and decorating the stage — six square platforms of varying heights — these we decorated with wild colors of crepe paper and put up a rail around them. I had asked the carpenter to make me some stilts, fancying that I could master same and march forth as the tallest lady in the world. Ha! That was a joke. I brought them back to my room to practice and proceeded to break my neck — almost. I could not strap them on properly but managed to get up on them by clutching the ceiling, walls, doors, anything within reach. Then I decided it was just too dangerous. There was no doubt about it — I would break my neck on stilts.

Other girls had done a superhuman job in a night and one morning of decorating the whole recreation room. Visitors would enter the room through a white cattle-swinging gate. In the middle was a square enclosure with sides of colored, fringed crepe paper over canvas. In this area was a bingo or game of chance. On one side was a bowling alley and along the wall opposite the stage and the wall at right angle were the various booths — wildly decorated. It did look like a circus or carnival and all but smelled of sawdust and elephants. Leta, our fat girl, is also an artist and on brown sheets of wrapping paper had painted the pictures of the sideshow freaks and these were hung in succession on the closed stage curtain.

Tickets to all the booths, etc., were given out to each man as he entered. We had been collecting thousands of little prizes for weeks and with packages of cigarettes, there were enough. One girl had a fishpond grab-bag booth. Those who did not get prizes received a little fish with a nonsense rhyme on the back.

COFFEE and SYMPATHY
World War II Letters from the Southwest Pacific

For us the most hysterical part of the sideshow was when I was stuffing pillows down Leta's very big blue bloomers and they split. Leta had curled her hair as the child Shirley Temple and painted her face like a doll. She did look like a dolly of the circus. I wore an old-fashioned gingham dress, very elongated, a weird curled red wig with a red bow and yellow flowers. I made myself up with much red splotchy rouge, eye shadow and wide lips. I looked like a made-up scarecrow. I stood on a box covered by the dress and placed myself on the highest platform. I read a love-story magazine and stood in a stooped position and bent from the waist.

Leta, the fat lady, or "Bubbles," ate chocolate candy all the time. Charlie Townes, snake charmer, is very gentle looking and feminine. She wore oriental attire. Another girl's face assumed very nicely a red beard for the bearded lady. She was in gaudy Byzantine attire and knitted constantly on a pale blue sweater. The two youngsters were adorable in blue grown-up evening clothes. Well, we stood there. A barker barked outside the curtain and the customers filed in. The barker used to bark for carnivals in Hollywood. He was very good.

The boys laughed and laughed at us. Some of them just accepted us and others wanted to see! I know I made an amazing impression and did look like the tallest lady in the world. However, if some wanted to spoil the illusion that was their fun. They guffawed at us and with us and heckled us. It was an exhausting performance. We had two showings of an hour each and then at the end we were part of the finale. The two midgets sang and danced. Another little girl did the same. Then the freaks paraded, the snake charmer wriggled a bit and the bearded lady came out. I walked out stiffly on high tiptoes and some people thought I was on stilts. Then Leta came out and sang, "Put Your Arms Around Me, Baby, Hold Me Tight" and she can really sing too. The two acrobats acrobatted and the boys all stood there jammed together and loved it. That was a good ending to the day. The booths still carried on a little while but it was over for us, thank goodness. Everyone had a marvelous time. Imagine popcorn and lemonade for perhaps 3,000 people! It was work but I think it was appreciated, so that makes it worth all the trouble.

It is now nearly 9 p.m. and I have to go out on the mobile canteen tonight. One of the girls is sick. I must get up at 2 a.m. and drive out to the airport to serve doughnuts and coffee to plane passengers.

The play was a hit. Everyone loved my green dress on stage. I am giving an honest and smooth performance.

I heard from Jim yesterday. He is waiting for his relief to come on leave.

Love,
Marcia

Marcia Ward Behr

[Brisbane]
July 10, 1944

Dearest Mother, Daddy and Family,

Thanks so much for your letter, Mother, which I received today. I am so glad you and Dad are having a long deserved vacation. Is Daddy not too well? You say he is dieting? That he cannot eat between meals. What does that mean?

When Jim comes I shall see if I can get a picture of him, either borrow a camera or make him get a commercial one. I can imagine you would like a view of him. I do hope he comes soon because I am going away. It all happened today, but the play will keep me here until August and it will be a couple of weeks after that. They asked us individually if we wanted to go North. They need personnel and new Red Cross workers are arriving from the States, so they are giving us old people a chance to go. I might just as well go and see what it is like. I pray Jim comes before I leave because I want to talk to him about New Guinea. I am glad now I took the part in the play because we have only two more performances this week and then do not perform again until the end of the month. Yes, I am keeping all reviews — one, to be exact. I feel quite sure that Jim will get here, so I am not going to stew about it. Everything happens for the best, n'est-ce pas?

Happy birthday, Mother darling. I shall send a cable but it will be late, I know.

I received a letter from Frank today. He is still in a Navy hospital but will be coming East soon and says he will call on the family. I think you will like him, although his table eating is not the best. I remember that, but he is a gentleman.

Do not worry about my latest move. Hilda Thompson must have eased you on that score. I won't need any more stockings now, nor shoes. My new uniform will be ready Wed. and I shall wear it all the time now.

> Love,
> Marcia

COFFEE and SYMPATHY
World War II Letters from the Southwest Pacific

[Brisbane]
July 18, 944

Dearest Family,

I hope there is not too long a wait in between this letter and the last. I never have too much heart to write when two weeks go by and I do not hear from Jim. I should realize mail is slow and irregular; besides, he must be a bit bored up there and there is not much he can say. I received two beautiful letters from him today. I tell him everything I do, in detail, as I tell you. He says, "It is quite right for you to go out, Marcia, and I really believe that it is the healthy thing to do. You are so far from home and if you can find enjoyment in other people, you should. I know that I am practically sawing my arm off, but I do know too that you love me and it is in that, that I find security. I really do not care about going out here because it is all superficial and it's too much trouble. That latter must sound eerie but mud, jeep, unfavorable entertaining facilities, the "leer" from the mob, the pseudo sophistication of the girls and the general attitude is just contrary to what one might expect. This place has changed so from the start when we landed in LSTs. It's on the verge of being a country club and it rather makes me ill. I will be so glad when orders take me into the scene of action again."

"I rather imagine that you and I think alike, Marcia. I love fun, beer, and have no end of gay moments. But it seems so darned out of place here that I cannot get over it. May the time come for a change."

"Your letters mean so much to me. I write as often as I can but the inconsistency must cause you to wonder a bit. It really should not, although it must be hard on you."

It is terribly late and I must go to bed now, but I have a lot more to tell you when I continue this tomorrow.

I met a Red Cross girl from the place where Jim is the other day and I asked her if she knew him. She said yes. He had come in to her club room one night with an ensign. She said both were very high and wanted her to go out. She also said he was married for a couple of years and now divorced and that he is from Connecticut. At first I was so glad to hear that she did know him, and then, like a sap, I began thinking about what she said. No mail from Jim and time to brood. I read his letters and they are sincere. It is funny how every time I wonder concerning Jim, a letter comes from him and answers my quandaries. The very next day I happened to be talking about the above girl with someone else and found that she likes to gossip anyway. I did not write to Jim for two or three days. I could not write anything but a gloomy letter. In his last before these last two, he said, "letters would flow now" that he is out of the hospital. It did not seem to me that he was writing at all. I wrote a good letter to find out what was happening. I had the feeling that he had not left the base. I know from other people what his base is like now and I know how bored people can get and that they search for little pleasures or escapes. Then these last two letters dispelled all doubts. The gist of my letter was that I wanted to keep writing every day if it gives him pleasure, but my ego or pride would keep me from wanting to bore him.

Jim says my letters read like a storybook and he can hardly wait for the next chapters. Wait until he hears that I am coming to New Guinea. He also said that his leave is still doubtful. Well, lately I have been preparing myself for such a disappointment. It seems all my life I have been looking way ahead for good things to happen and I am still looking.

I was so happy with his letters that it must have shown in my face. I was leaving the club to go home when a very beautiful, frail, blond girl in New Guinea khakis, stopped me in the lobby. I heard her say to her shorter companion: "This girl will tell us." She wanted to know where the staff dining room was. She said she asked me because I was the only girl around she had seen with a grin on her face. She seemed annoyed with the whole club and probably thanked her lucky stars that she had been sent north right away. I told her I was going there. and she said, "You'll love it." She has been up north eight months and has never been on the mainland. She landed in New Guinea and is now down on leave, I presume.

Sunday I was in the library and looked up to answer a voice asking if I had *Gone With the Wind*? You could have heard my heart stop for a minute. It was Jim Bothwell! [He was the brother of a very dear friend.] He was only here for the night on his way to Sydney and then back up north to find his ship, a cruiser. He is a full lieutenant. He had just been in Garden City three months ago. I left the club at 5:30 and went with him and some of his friends from the ship that transported him down here from New Guinea, and we went to the American Center. Just as we walked in the door we bumped into Don Weadon. I think I mentioned that he came up and spoke to me when I was on leave. Don is a major now. He is really a grown-up man and I feel as though he is older than I am. We had some beer at beer call, and then Jim Bothwell and Don and someone else and I had dinner downstairs. Don impressed me immensely. He stated that he thinks most people in Garden City [where I grew up] are dull and, if they are not, they get out. He expresses himself very well and, apparently, does a lot of thinking. He is one man in the Army who likes his job and also conducts himself rationally regarding his social life.

Jim and I talked and talked about home and family. He is a wonderful boy and I felt so close to home and past life and childhood. He said that everybody in Garden City is restless and anxious to do more for the war. I am really glad that I am overseas. Even if I could scream at moments. At least I understand how everyone else feels in this war and I am very close to the persons actually participating. I must write to Betty and tell her all about her brother Jim.

Last night I went with a goon to hear *The Gondoliers* put on by the same company as did *The Pirates* in Sydney. It was an excellent production. And on Sunday I saw Judith Anderson [a great Broadway star]. A morale boost.

Love,
Marcia

[Brisbane]
July 24

Dearest Family,

Buying and gathering and selecting clothes for New Guinea takes up most of my free time now. It gives me the same feeling as when I joined the Red Cross. It is the mystery of the adventure which interests me. I have heard so much about life up there but it is still hard to know what it is really like, so now I shall see for myself. The Red Cross almost insists that I take a leave before I go, but I do not need one. I am not tired and I look rested. I am still thin but much fatter than I was in Cairns. I think I look very well and I pray that I shall have the enthusiasm to do the job up there. I do hope they send me as far forward as possible. Never fear, my dears, they never send women to a place until it is quite civilized. The military takes care of us very well indeed and it is true that women can be dreadfully spoiled over here, unless you remember the theory of supply and demand.

I am so glad that Sergeant Rocque called. He is a nice little person. I knew him in Cairns. He was the supply sergeant and I used to get the Filipinos cigarettes and shoes, etc. from him. The Filipinos were like helpless, grasping children and Rocky was very understanding and patient. He had been over here a long time, first in New Guinea and then for a year in Cairns. Don't let him kid you. I do not have so many men after me but then I am only interested in one. It is really safer and better that way. Actually, it is a protection for me and sometimes I am very thankful for it — on my time off I want to do what rests and amuses me, not go out with just anybody.

I just love my G.I. shoes. I tried on everything last night.

I am going to have library duty most of this week. That is where I am now. A whole pack of new magazines came in the other day and it makes this room so much nicer to see gay-colored interesting magazines around.

Yesterday we gave a tea and reception for the volunteer workers, those girls who come to dances, social affairs and outings. It was very nice indeed. I helped serve and wore my new uniform, hat, white shirt and gloves. My new suit is very attractive and of lovely material, dark grey blue woolen gabardine and fits just beautifully. I shall take it to New Guinea with me where it will probably rot and get covered with blue mold. My black shoes are absolutely worn out and I have about one pair of rayon stockings left, so I just have to get out of here quickly.

I hope I can find a stamp and mail this today.

All my love,
Marcia

[Brisbane]
July 28, 1944

Dearest Family,

I received two letters from Jim and in the first he said he was definitely coming on leave in about five weeks. I doubt if I am still here if transportation is available. In the second he was quite excited about my coming to New Guinea, but only if I can come to his location. Well, of course that would be marvelous and I am going to the island partly on the chance of seeing him. Really it is getting to the point where we should see each other. It is almost a year now.

He told me about a terrific wind and rainstorm they were having and huge trees falling on tents injuring and killing people. When you get near the equator, nature stirs itself in a very weird fashion.

I was annoyed this morning when reading one of the girls' letters from New Guinea. She passed her opinion on those girls who should and should not go to New Guinea — said "no" for me, that I should be in a more civilized and charming place. Well, I have done my own washing before and used outdoor privies for a year and suffered many tropical bugs and driven army trucks over pretty rough roads and, looking back on that time, this club is torture by comparison — just like working in a subway all day long. If this is charming civilization, give me New York. I suppose everyone thinks of me as a soft lady but you at least know me better. At any rate, I am going to New Guinea. It would not be the way of living which would bother me but what the boys willy-nilly think of the girls. They adopt a very disrespectful attitude. They think we are carrying on with everyone — only date officers and that the A.R.C. is a racket — and that we joined it for men, wine and song. Knowing that beforehand may help but, being sensitive, I suppose it may bother me. However, I have my self-respect and truth is truth no matter what anyone thinks.

My cholera shot took effect last night and I had chills. I went to bed at 7 p.m. It must have been that because I seem to be all right today.

All my love,
Marcia

[Brisbane]
August 5, 1944

Dearest Aunt Mary,

Happy birthday to you! Perhaps too soon, but I do hope not too late. Mail is very hard to time these days. I shall probably be somewhere in New Guinea to celebrate my birthday. I shall think of you on that day and mentally drink a toast to you.

I am quite sure the jungle heat will not bother me. They say it is sometimes hotter in Cairns than in New Guinea. I rather thrive on hot weather and shrivel and shake in cold weather. Actually, the climate here in Brisbane in the winter season is wonderful — brisk, cool, clear sunny days, and nights are quite cold — very good for sleeping. The only trouble is that indoor heat is non-existent; so, if you are not in the sun or not in bed under two or three blankets, you are cold. Our club is the largest service club in this theatre-of-war and it is like a barn all the time. The masses of people help to warm it, but I still wear plenty of sweaters and warm underwear. I believe it starts getting really warm here again about the first of October.

I have never been in the so-called rainy season. It was late this year in Cairns and I left before I had more than a week of it. However, I hear that it literally rains all the time in New Guinea and that the mud is preposterous. I shall have to wear khaki pants and G.I. heavy, high shoes all the time. Lots of people are very discouraging about my going north, others rave about the place. The boys especially tell me I am crazy to go, but I am curious. I can brave the elements. I shall try to keep as clean and well-groomed as possible because I believe that is important.

My present location is a rather large city with nothing particularly to recommend it as far as I can see. There are ten wonderful beaches fairly close and a few mountain resorts where I have never been. The architecture is typical of most tropical Australia — wooden bungalows on stilts. Naturally, there are many modern buildings, but the place has no quaintness or particular atmosphere. It was interesting for me to work in this large club in a leave area. It helps to complete the picture. I worked with men untouched by battle in Cairns who were still maneuvering. Down here men are on leave from combat, and I expect up there I shall feel much closer to the war, though always at a safe distance. New Guinea is a much more habitable and civilized place than it was ten months ago.

Mother's letters assure me that all is well at home. The election of the president must be the all absorbing issue on the home front. I sent for a ballot which will probably arrive too late, as it did last year. They should really give overseas people a chance to vote.

All my love and happiness to you on your birthday,

Marcia

[Brisbane]
Aug. 5, 1944

Dearest Family,

I received your letter today written June 30. The mail is screwy — talked about going to Jamesport, L. I., and was mostly from Sylvia. Both Syl and Nan sound very gay. I am so glad. For heaven's sake, wait until I get home before you have another wedding. It is bad enough to have to miss one.

No letter from Jim today, so I really do not know what is happening to him. I wonder if he is still coming on leave. I keep writing to him and try to make the letters interesting because he does appreciate them. The only thing is, I may be leaving tomorrow morning and then I won't hear from him for ages because of the change in A.P.O. Syl made me laugh saying she will die if Jim and I do not get together soon. Imagine how I feel. I never seem to go about anything the easy way. It certainly ought to be good when everything works out. I am not only working at the thing. Jim is trying too and with two people fighting in the same direction, that should make the objective more secure.

I am not feeling too well this afternoon but I shall go out to the hospital to see a colonel who is in a closed ward, I shall make faces through the window. He heard I was in Brisbane and called to ask me to come out and see him. He was wounded in the north somewhere.

I would really rather not go tomorrow. I will call at five today to find out the answer and let you know before sending this letter. I am going to church now and then come back and wash clothes and my hair.

Love,
Marcia

Marcia Ward Behr

New Guinea

It was August 10, 1944, when I finally landed at Oro Bay on the coast of Papua New Guinea. The area swarmed with khaki-clothed military personnel flying in and out on various missions. A former jungle village, captured along with Buna in January 1943, had been transformed into a sophisticated Army base. Newly built social clubs offered relaxation and refreshments, and there was a well-equipped and staffed hospital. The crushed coral roads led to military bases and airports some distance away; jeeps and trucks everywhere raised choking dust.

The Red Cross women were accommodated in a huge dorm-like tent where there was just a cot to call your own. At 4:30 every morning I would get up, dress, and shine my flashlight as I walked to the gate of the compound — the rats scattering before me away from the light. A sergeant met me in a jeep, and we had a long dusty ride to the airfield where we prepared the coffee and sandwiches for the crews of the planes continuously taking off and returning.

Red Cross girls and sandwiches were synonymous in the islands whether we were in a canteen, meeting the paratroopers after practice jumps, visiting camps, or driving jeeps up and down the airstrips stopping to give refreshments to passengers on hospital planes, to pilots and crews, or to the men working on the planes in the broiling equator sun. Cold drinks were favored on sunny days but coffee always when it rained.

Sometimes I used to think it was just the refreshment that the boys appreciated, and women shouldn't have been in this man's world. Any G.I. could hand out the food and drinks. I was wrong. There was such a thing as a woman's touch being different. The Army mess did not serve chow daintily to a line of hungry soldiers. A young Red Cross woman would seem to be dishing out strawberry shortcake for dessert instead of canned peaches. Though dressed in khakis and G.I. shoes, I symbolized a rare dish in that rough setting. When I turned the spigot at the airport canteen, we shared a moment of social grace without conversation. It was as though, serving at a tea party, I smiled and offered the drink. He took it saying "Thank you" and I responded with "You're welcome."

Naturally, we were eager to move closer to the combat area which was now 1100 miles northwest from Oro Bay. However, we had to wait until the Army could make a newly captured island ready (latrines, showers and a fenced compound) for the Red Cross workers.

While I remained at Oro Bay, the Allies captured Peleliu and Ulithi, two islands important for a clear passage to the Philippines.

[Oro Bay]
August 12, 1944

Dearest Family,

I am in New Guinea. I am not where I would like to be but perhaps a period of waiting will prove profitable.

We had a good trip by flying boat most of the way. It took just two days, stopped over night at Cairns. It is very quiet and quite deserted. The Red Cross Club is still open in town because there is some Navy there. Charlie Townes and I came up together. She is a charming girl from Baltimore and we are together now.

We spent one night at a place in New Guinea which is very civilized [Port Moresby]; it even has houses. There is an Allied Officers Club that is quite famous in these parts. It is a natively-built bamboo building hanging out over the harbor. Here one can get a most delicious dinner with white tablecloths, napkins and all the dishes and trimmings. It is served by natives wearing gay colored skirts and flowers in their bushy black hair. An orchestra plays sweet music all through dinner and there is dancing every night until 10 p.m. The menu is all numbered so you tell the waiter the numbers desired and hence no language complication.

It is a bit incongruous to see nurses and A.R.C. girls dressed in khaki slacks dancing and dining in this very swank and atmospheric place. Naturally we were also in pants.

The Red Cross girls at the above place were very hospitable and took us to the Allied Club for both lunch and dinner and let us use their little cottage with all freedom. There are about three cottages where the Red Cross girls live and they are completely surrounded by a high barbed-wire fence and an M.P. guard — a necessary precaution, it seems. To date at night one must go with two couples and an armed officer as a necessary precaution. There is nothing to fear but women must be protected.

A.P.O. 503 [Oro Bay] where we are now is called the garden spot of New Guinea. It is very pretty and right on the ocean front. There are roads and roads all over the place and the dirt and dust seems to me a great inconvenience. If you drive anywhere, the traffic kicks up dust and you are simply black upon arrival at any destination. It is cooler here than summertime in Cairns and one always needs a blanket at night.

Our period spent on the mainland means nothing up here. We have no priority whatsoever over girls who have been here in New Guinea longer than we but who perhaps left the States a year after we did. That was a blow because upon our arrival we had hopes of going to more exciting areas. The outlook of this place seems very dull.

It is a very restricted life. In fact to have a date or any social life is such a lot of trouble that it is hardly worth the effort. Charlie and I got cornered into a dance last night. We drove for miles and miles in an open jeep and arrived as described above. We do not care if we ever see our escorts again and were really glad when we got back to our quarters. We just made the midnight curfew. The ride back was a terrific strain due to the shortness of time.

They have put us up at a hospital a few miles away from the A.R.C. setup. Here life is made very comfortable for the Army nurses — screened in barracks, two people to a room — immaculate showers and outdoor plumbing. There are sewing rooms and washing facilities of the most modern variety. The nurses and all of us do all our own washing and time off is utilized to a great extent in the care and upkeep of personal belongings. Charlie and I have been quite happy discovering the joys of a washing machine and starching and ironing our G.I. trousers and safari jackets. The latter we have been bleaching. Each one comes out a different shade. Mine turned out bright orange.

I have not known what to about the Atabrine situation but since it is an Army regulation I have taken one a day as per order. You have probably read about this malaria depressive. It makes people yellow but one's pigment returns to normal after consumption ceases.

I do not know what has been happening to Jim. Of course, I am a little discouraged about when I shall see him. I hope to hear from him soon.

I just stopped for a moment to put on one of my pretty nightgowns and the blue princess negligee I bought in Sydney. I feel better now.

So far I think the food has been quite good. We had fresh eggs for breakfast and fresh meat last night — lamb, and rabbit twice today, fresh potatoes the last two nights and today I ate my first dehydrated potatoes. Of course, one never sees fresh fruit or vegetables and I suppose they are a rare treat.

We left the hospital for work at 8 a.m. Charlie is helping out in the area office doing some typing. They are very short of secretaries, in fact have none. Charlie broke the typewriter right away. Must have been something wrong with it.

I am doing clubmobile work. It is very easy. We fill cans with ice cold drinks and pack cakes and cookies to put in the mobile truck. A detail of soldiers does all the lifting and the driving. Two girls go along for the dusty ride. Once there, the boys unload and we turn the spigot to fill the boys' cups as they file past. The other girl serves the cake. We say "you're welcome" all the time and look up with a grin. After the repast we stand around and talk. This is enjoyable and quite satisfactory as the boys seem very appreciative; it only takes about an hour altogether. We go to all the different camps and seldom go back to the same place twice. There are two clubmobiles and they go out once in the morning and afternoon.

I found I knew several of the Red Cross girls stationed here. They all want to go farther north. It is too regimented here and all the fun has gone out of it. I do think New Guinea could get along without any women at all but I am glad to be seeing it for myself. The living conditions are certainly not at all rugged. I imagine keeping up with one's own washing is the most exhausting part of the deal but, with everyone in the same boat, it is not so bad.

I feel that if I serve a limited amount of time here, the way things move so quickly, I may be rewarded before long with a change for the better. One can be so popular here that it is not even flattering. Do not fear that I shall be a spoiled little girl. If I can be a queen dressed in orange, you know things are slightly distorted. As a matter of fact, I think we were more popular on the mainland, Australia. We looked better anyway.

I left Brisbane Tuesday morning, August 8th. I shall try to write more very soon. I am a bit sleepy now although it is only 10 p.m., but we have to get up at 7 and eat breakfast by 7:30.

All my love,
Marcia

[Oro Bay]
August 18, 1944

Dearest Family,

I am working two nights this week. Last night some of us went to an Ordnance Corps dance. We are not permitted to date enlisted men but this was a specially arranged occasion. There were about twenty Wacs there and five of us. I danced and danced until I thought it would never end. These boys have been overseas for nearly three years and lots of them, I suppose, have not been to a dance in a good long time or even talked to any girls. It was really good to see the pleasure it gave the boys and was worth a lot to all of us.

Charlie and I both feel, though, that in order to arouse our enthusiasm once again, we need a little responsibility and to be put in an interesting spot, not in a base a thousand miles behind the lines. That is our gripe.

I visited a native village last Sunday — thatched houses on stilts, black people with bushy hair squatting and some painting on materials, others smoking but mostly just sitting with the little children, their bellies puffed out from malaria, running every which way. We said "good day" and they reciprocated constantly. They smiled — some with beautiful white teeth and some with black teeth from chewing betel nuts.

I suppose all the villages are somewhat alike and this one looked just like the photographs I had seen. The natives love to peroxide their hair and every other one has a curly, bushy, crop of reddish-blond hair. They mostly wear just a dash of material around their hips and both sexes are nude from the waist up. The Aussies used to get a day's work out of them for one cigarette butt. I suppose we Yanks with our exuberant generosity have spoiled them. The natives jump for joy at the gift of a tin of bully beef. Of course, some natives have been very well schooled at the missions and speak good English and one can never belittle their knowledge of the jungle. They must think foreigners are very dumb about the New Guinea terrain and wildlife.

Charlie and I are still out at the hospital but expect to be moving soon to the mission where most of the girls stay. I am going on a run this afternoon and we shall probably serve drinks and cakes to about 1500 men. I do not need anything sent to me because I can buy most everything here. I sent a footlocker home. Please save my plaid suit.

Love,
Marcia

[Oro Bay]
8-22-44

Dearest Family,

Apparently, I am acquiring a certain recognition of any small efforts in my present work and Barna, my director, said she would write a report about me before I leave. They have given me the responsibility of the canteen out at the airport. Any Rosy O'Grady could do the job. There are not too many planes but, when they come in we have a very rushing business and I hardly have time to say, "you're welcome." We boil the water outside in a garbage can with a gas heating contraption stuck inside and make the coffee in a 20-gallon boiler on a field range.

Aug. 23 — We had a huge business today. During the hours of 7:00 a.m. and 1:00 p.m., we served 30 gallons of coffee and used 25 loaves of bread. I have a detail of four soldiers and they are very sweet and helpful. Their sandwich production is amazing. In no time they whip up huge platefuls. I keep busy pouring the coffee and seeing that cream, sugar and sandwich plates are full and that the place is clean and swept and generally boss the outfit. We are a happy group and, although the work is physically demanding, I am glad to be busy.

Back bases are so G.I. and for lack of things to do, restrictions are added constantly. It is a hardship to go out and so I am always avoiding it. I try to be pleasant at all times but there is a weight on my heart. If I were only in a more interesting place.

I have not heard from Jim in almost a month and this does worry me. When I am busy and working, it is better. It is not so easy to arouse myself to enjoy going out with other people. Mr. Anthony [newspaper columnist], what shall I do?

Barna, my present director, has been very good to me and is going to put in her report a recommendation that I be the first sent north from here. That is encouraging.

I received a letter from you written at Jamesport with Syl's letter enclosed.

All my love to everyone.

Love,
Marcia

P.S. I am not taking Atabrine.

[Oro Bay]
August 25, 1944

My dearest sister Sylvia,

I am so very thrilled for you. I just cannot believe it. You must be in seventh heaven. I am simply dying to meet your Jack Juraschek. When I received your letter I wept. I was so homesick and just cannot bear the thought of missing your wedding I want to be there so much.

This is a very exciting life but I am tired of this war, aren't you? I know how you must miss Jack when he is gone. I want to come home but as long as I think I might see Jim, I shall stay. I hear that his base may have moved. He is quite far north from me [in fact Milne Bay is a few hundred miles southeast], but even his base is way back of being forward now. I heard last night that I can telephone there. The operator said he would try to reach the base, but the lines were out. If I could reach the place, perhaps I could find out whether he is there or not. I know that he is a fine person and very sincere, but there are many abnormal occurrences in wartime and the fact that people are so long separated is difficult. Jim would not be unfair in any way. It must be that he cannot write.

It was two days ago that I started this letter. Now it is my day off and I am so hot in this tent that my hand sticks to the paper. Someone gave me some pictures that he took at Yorkies Knob and here is one of me wearing a dress I found in Innisfail, a town about 60 miles south of Cairns.

All my love and happiness to you and Jack. What bliss!

Your loving sister,
Marcia

[Milne Bay]
August 29, 1944

Dear Marcia,

This is a rush note to say "sit tight" and keep your chin up. I think something will happen before too long. Finally, yesterday I got to talk with Doug Baldwin. Doug says to tell you that you're on his "horse trading" list. The truth, not to be told out, is that he had already requested you and two or three others, none of whom he got. His feeling was that the setup there seems to work negatively on all such requests, but I think he made enough of a fuss with Bob that he may be able to work it. Doug is very much in favor of you and there's just a very vague hunch I have that Doug may be able to work one of the first Philippine assignments and you and I could go with him. We, half-jokingly, but seriously, said we were going to make the first team for the first Navy base there.

It was like coming home when I joined the base the first of April having spent three weeks getting nowhere with the Army. I swear I'm a Navy girl from here on.

As for knowing Jim Wilder — I sure do. I first kidded him when he was in the hospital with a beautiful pair of black eyes after a jeep accident. Then I had him looking out for Bill's flattop. Remember my Bill, back in Washington and the one day I got to see him? The ship brought him out here after so many months, and for 24 hours they lay off the coast, came into the stream so close I could almost swim out, but he could not get on shore, nor I on ship, even with the persuasions of our captain here. It was sad! Now there's little hope of his coming in here again.

I had two mighty rugged spots and this is heaven.

So, keep the chin up — she'll be right!

Love,
Connie [Red Cross girl]

[Oro Bay]
Sept. 3, 1944

Dearest Family,

I can imagine you are all involved in the wedding plans. It would be nice to be there. Tell Jack that I am just dying to meet the one who won Sylvia's heart. She has always been pretty particular and he must be sumpin'. Please buy yourselves a nice wedding present from me.

The other day we went to a native dance festival. It reminded me of Gallup, N.M. They get all dressed up and paint their faces and beat drums and make rhythmical noises and dance. We passed out refreshments to the soldier-spectators and then saw some of the dancing ourselves. The Papuans are not as colorful or exciting to watch as our Indians. It is amazing to see such a big city here of modern Army life and equipment and then, just a little way into the jungle, the native laborers revert to their native celebrations.

I imagine that it would be fascinating to walk back in the jungle. They do look so impregnable — tall trees centuries old tower into the sky and the leafage and foliage tangling at the roots look very weird and mysterious. Suddenly a beautiful flower sticks up. However, I do not think I would care to pervade the jungles without a good guide, and then there is typhus and malaria to be avoided.

I am not worrying about getting these diseases. In fact, I have not been taking Atabrine as I should according to Army regulations. I try to feel that I am protected.

If you are worrying about false popularity going to my head, please do not. It is becoming a game with me to see just how much I can stay home and not go out. I imagine Cairns spoiled me because there were so many attractive people there who were simpatico and who seemed to like me for myself and not just because I was a girl among so many men.

It was cold enough last night for four blankets but it is very hot again today. I just had a glass of cold milk someone brought off a ship. I have not had any for a month. We never get fresh fruit or vegetables. We get fresh meat and potatoes once in awhile. However the food is not too bad and I eat quite enough. I do eat a lot of peanut butter and jam.

Hilda Thompson is in Sydney. She is dying to get back up here, but I think she would find it quite different. In fact, New Guinea is very civilized now. I cannot say it is the most exciting place in the world. Jim's letter has not come yet. I have faith and so I go on hopefully from day to day. Such is life.

Much love to all,
Marcia

[Solomon Islands]
Sept. 8, 1944

Hello, Marcia!

It was rather surprising to hear of your arrival in God's forsaken land. I always thought that only us unfortunate individuals were sent to the islands as punishment but now that they are sending you over there I am beginning to doubt it.

I wish I could have seen you if it actually was you that I saw going toward the beach; we would have had a swell time at the club, but then it always happens the way we don't want it to. When you arrive, we leave. I'll be looking forward to seeing you in the Philippines, if I don't see you before then.

One of the American officers I met at the Intelligence School lived in Manila where his father has a mansion, and from what one of the men in the company told me it is a palatial place. He had visited it several times while his dad was stationed in Manila. As I started to say, I have a date there with him unless I am sent home on rotation or wounded. I think I'd prefer to go home in one piece.

I know how you feel about the island because we had felt the same but then we had so much work to do that the inconveniences were forgotten and only the bunk looked good. Naturally, upon our arrival last August before the Nadzab [in Papua New Guinea] deal we were certainly at a loss. After being spoiled on the mainland for such a long period of time, we were all hurting, but since we knew what was in the wind, we forgot everything except that one thing.

Those dusty roads are really a hindrance, especially when you try to stay clean. I can just imagine how hard it is for you to try to take care of your clothes, hair and body riding along the "highways."

It would be really swell to have you come up here where we are because girls are very, very scarce on this island; in fact, there are none here. In fact, we have seen only two girls, white, since we left Oro Bay last June. If you were here about two weeks ago, you would have had to live in a jungle hammock among the trees here, but now we are becoming civilized once more. We are living in tents and sleep on cots. When we leave the spot it will be an ideal island of paradise — if you can call a coral atoll a land of paradise.

I didn't realize that they had so many of you girls in one tent. At present we have only four men in ours, while back in Oro Bay I lived with one other officer in a tent built up off the ground with a wooden floor, electric lights and running water. My tent was situated on the bank of a creek that was cool and rapid. Since it was a fairly steep bank, we found a set of stairs and placed them into the creek connecting our tent. It was just like home except for one thing. The little woman.

I think that it would be best if you could get with a hospital because a girl as sweet as you could really cheer a fellow up when he is feeling low. I remember a remark one of the men made when I asked him if he had seen you at the Red Cross in Brisbane. He asked me if I meant the girl with that swell smile; he said that he hadn't seen you at any time without a smile.

There is a slight possibility of my being sent back there where you are. Several days ago I had requested a transfer to the paratroop outfit that is located there because as long as I am in this outfit I will not get anywhere, so I had requested a change. The colonel approved and I am only waiting to hear from Sixth Army.

Tell Kay Irving that I'll tell Andy Kitt to write her. He is rather busy and I can't locate him but just as soon as I do I'll tell him. You know he was wounded in the first real skirmish we had here. It wasn't a serious wound, just a few shrapnel in his arm and leg. His platoon was in the lead when they were hit and they really did a good job on the Nips.

Keep smiling, Marcia, and don't pick up that Atabrine tan.

Take care of yourself.

                Sincerely,
                Chet

Marcia Ward Behr

[Oro Bay]
Sept. 13, 1944

Dearest Family,

I may not be able to finish this now as I have to go to a dance.

I am always getting involved in social engagements which bore me stiff. I try not to have any. I am enclosing some mail I received today and think you might enjoy reading. Connie was with me in Washington. We always planned to be together.

Theo Kilburn, a new girl, very attractive, a Smith graduate, lives in New Haven and worked for Powers in an administrative job in New York City, and I are very happy together. We have been given charge of the airstrip canteen and it is better than anything else around here. Her best beau is Air Corps. He is someone from home whom she has not seen in two years. He flies bombers and attack planes. He came to see her and offered to take me to see Jim. So that is how it happened. Only a little more than half an hour's ride and so wonderful. Betty, another girl who knew someone up there, and I rode in front and could see everything so clearly.

We arrived about 1 p.m. to return at 2 p.m. I called Jim and he said he would be right out. The other girl's beau came right out. I waited an hour — no Jim. I had not told him specifically enough where to come. I called his office and they said he had come but given up thinking I had to leave right away. They said he had gone off the base, but would try to find him, though they sounded discouraging. I was most miserable, such luck. I called back in ten minutes. Jim was on the wire. It was 2:30 then. Of course the others said they would wait. He came.

Now it is like a dream. It was too quick. I wonder what he thought. We talked naturally and laughed. There was no strain, but I had gone through so much emotion before, that I don't remember my reactions. He does not get many of my letters and said that he has written more than I ever receive.

He might come to see me. He wants me to put on the pressure to go home. To see him again for one day would be so important to me and I think to him too.

Note the date on Connie's letter. It takes two weeks. She is at Jim's base.

I went to Harry Corwin, the director of personnel, and asked him to please get me out of here. I mentioned Jim's place or farther north. He said he would get me out soon. In a few days I shall go to him again.

COFFEE and SYMPATHY
World War II Letters from the Southwest Pacific

There was an A.R.C. dance the other night and I was in the fashion show. This sounds very minor but to me it was most significant in a personal way. It completely revived my faith in myself as an actress which *The Women* did not.

The first part was straight but ridiculous, because it showed the suitable dresses to wear for sport, tea, cocktails, dining and dancing at the various A.R.C. clubs around here. The girl who did the announcing put on a French accent and her script was clever. The orchestra played suitable music. The second half was a complete caricature. First a girl came on in pajamas, helmet, gas mask, leggings and toothbrush. She was dressed for crossing from our barracks to showers.

To explain: 83 new A.R.C. girls and a number of U.S.O. actresses descended upon the base about a week ago. Some barracks were thrown up in two days but with no plumbing, water or facilities whatever; the girls would have to walk 200 yards outside their compound and cross over to ours to use our toilets and showers. Simply a madhouse! (I have a most tremendous amount of dirty clothes and do not know when I shall ever be able to squeeze through the mob and to grab a pail to wash them.) So the M.P. would stop the women and make them go back for their leggings because they should be wearing them at all times after dark outside the compounds.

Another model demonstrated how a girl can use her imagination when wearing fatigues for a hard day's work at the club. She wore earrings, a red bandeau, high-heeled shoes, a gay belt and carried a broom. Then I was asked to model my Sydney negligee — you know that blue georgette princess-like gown that I bought in a rash moment when on leave. Of all things I packed it in my suitcase to bring up here and it is very ridiculous for camp life. I was to demonstrate certain necessary beauty restorative measures after hard work in New Guinea. I wore it over my G.I. pants and shoes. It was an improvisational performance as I had not been to any rehearsals. They handed me a G.I. scrubbing brush and a dust brush for props. Well, I drooped on the stage and you know how I can completely sag. I walked around like a sad sack and then took the center of the stage. I looked in a fake mirror and used the dust brush to vigorously brush my hair, then started on my complexion with the large scrub brush. Oh yes, first I did a luxurious yawn and stretch, then I bent over with a very straight back and did a Martha Graham contortion, then pulled out a handkerchief and with fanfare like a magician I placed it so — on the floor — and proceeded to do a headstand, spreading my feet apart and waving them in the air. I stood up and, from sheer and real exhilaration, let out a laughing shout and beat my chest with enthusiasm and walked gracefully to my corner. Naturally, everyone laughed and I knew I still had it in me. So that was an interesting little experience, most important to my inner self.

Theo said today she went to see Mr. Corwin. She told him how wonderful I am and how experienced, which is a lot of noise. She said we make a good team and have organized and fixed up the canteen, so that any two girls can take over in a hurry. She said we want to go north! He said Marcia wants to go to Milne Bay. She said, "Oh, no, she doesn't. Marcia would take that, but prefers a more exciting one. Jim will soon be leaving Milne Bay. So Mr. Corwin put our names together on a piece of paper and told Theo to be a good girl."

I wish I could get a letter from Jim and read his thought. As you say, I am bound to do the right thing and find my place.

All happiness and love,
Marcia

P.S. This pen is very difficult. I gave my good one to Jim.

[Oro Bay]
Sept. 19, 1944

Dearest Family,

The great event for Syl and Jack must be approaching with gathering momentum.

I have been weighing my situation. I am now going to be mercenary. If I come home, I shall have to find some kind of a remunerative job and just what could that be? If you can type, you can be hired, but I do not type and the thing I do best is act. You know how much that signifies commercially. Now I am doing something that is useful although I am not quite in my right niche where I could be the most helpful; I believe a little more time will improve the situation. At any rate I am next in line to go forward. I composed a letter of resignation but neither Charlie nor Theo would let me send it.

Jim's letters do not come through at all. Of course, I am completely out of Navy circulation here and that may be the trouble with the mail. I have not heard a word since I saw him. I write him just as often as I can.

We have been giving the fashion show at various camps and at each place I improve my act. They like it and I am funny and I do have fun doing it.

Theo and I have made a very good thing out of the canteen at the airstrip. It is very attractive. We managed to scrounge paint. It is red, white, blue and orange. The awning is red and white. Some twenty men are coming Sunday to landscape. The coffee is excellent and the reputation of the place is spreading. That is satisfying. I am a fiend for scrubbing and keeping the canteen clean.

The enclosed picture shows Theo and me visiting a Negro regiment.

                                    Love,
                                    Marcia

[Oro Bay]
Sept. 25, 1944

Dearest Family,

Still not having heard from Jim in all this time, I was thinking of planning without consideration of him. I just could not understand never getting any more mail.

Yesterday Mr. Eaton came to the airstrip to meet a passenger and told me where he would probably send me. It is quite far up on an island. There are a group of A.R.C. girls there now. As far as excitement, attention and good living quarters are concerned, they have it all.

I think I wrote you that I took a letter of resignation to Mr. Eaton and before I knew it he had promised to send me north right away. That was about five days ago and I let it ride until yesterday when he named the spot. Jim did say very definitely to put on the pressure to go home when I saw him for ten minutes two weeks ago. He would not be getting home for at least five months and probably a whole lot longer.

I kept thinking last night if only I could hear from him, just one letter. I thought of calling him, then I decided not to chase him and perhaps it is better not to write any more. And then I would think about him and what kind of a person he is and I could not believe that he would just plain stop writing. However, I decided not to write him very much.

I was listening to the radio last night and the war news was so good and I thought, I am certainly leaving just at the most interesting time. All day I found myself not too pleased with my resignation. I would wonder what was happening over here. Though I want to get home and see you all and enjoy home life, with the war still on and everyone away, I would feel pretty much out of things. There is no reason why, if I keep trying to do the right thing, I should not be protected from harm, sickness, or getting tired. This job assignment is an exciting one where we can do work that is appreciated.

Charlie Townes is going with me to the island [Biak].

                                    All my Love,
                                    Marcia

Marcia Ward Behr

Biak

The Red Cross sent me to the island of Biak, and it was all I had hoped. Biak, in what was then the Netherlands East Indies and is now Indonesia, lies 1,100 miles northwest of Oro Bay.

We lived high on a coral cliff overlooking the sea, protected inside a small fenced compound, four to a tent. Each of us had her own jeep for delivering our homemade sandwiches and lemonade to the weary returning airmen and the infantry troops awaiting the next invasion.

We arrived on September 29, 1944, just three months after the Japanese had evacuated. The Allies had already turned Biak into a supply depot and jumping-off place for the invasion of the Philippines. Each morning at dawn hundreds of bombers took off on missions, and we slept through the roar as the planes rose into the air right over our tents.

Here on Biak I could really feel the war and men in combat. Borneo and the Philippines were being bombed daily by B24s and B25s based on the island.

The Red Cross would call to get the estimated arrival time of the returning bombers, and we would meet the crew and pilots with a cold drink. They were tired boys. I would watch them come into the briefing room one by one. "Is there any mail for me?" When there was, I didn't think they looked so tired any more. They would go over and tell the story of the mission to the intelligence officer and then hold out their hands for a drink. Some would want to laugh and talk, and others would just grin and say "thank you." Everyone thanked you.

The infantrymen on Biak were seasoned warriors from several New Guinea battles. The enemy used the caves as fortresses. They lived there with tons of rice and ammunition. They let our soldiers and Marines come on the island for three days. Then the cave-dwellers blasted our men on the beaches. It took three months of hard fighting to secure Biak.

In spite of the Red Cross being so close to the war, and since all destinations were secret, we really had no idea where the action was or what was going on in the battle area. I realize now that the Air Force, along with the most powerful naval fleet then assembled, was poised to fight the battle of Leyte Gulf in the Philippines. From the grim faces of the airmen we visited with our jeep-canteens, we knew that they had been in a grueling battle. I feel sure that Jim Wilder's LST ship was ready to take part in the Leyte Island beach landings.

COFFEE and SYMPATHY
World War II Letters from the Southwest Pacific

On Christmas day of 1944, the Japanese surrendered Leyte Island. That night I went to the movies on Biak with friends. A short time after I returned to the States, I read in the news that a Japanese Kamikaze pilot had just bombed that same outdoor theater during the showing of a film and killed forty Americans.

From Leyte the next conquest for the Allies would be Manila on the island of Luzon. By July 5, 1945, all the Philippine Islands had been liberated, and these strategic lands became a staging area for the final moves against Japan.

[Biak]
September 28, 1944

Dearest Family,

At last I think Charlie and I have found a good place. At least I feel very, very happy and we both have felt that way since we stepped off the plane. This seems to be a place where the boys need us and want us. Actually, Charlie and I will be the first ones to open our new spot. We will be commuting by air from this island where we landed until our island base has built facilities for us.

We had a wonderful plane ride up here and saw a great deal of the terrain. One valley in particular was very beautiful with sloping hills that appeared to be covered with soft shades of brown, green and yellow velvet. The flat land was lusciously fertile-looking. Many native villages were scattered throughout.

I imagine the food will be a little better up here but I eat as much as ever anyway and, so my weight stays the same — about 115 lbs. You will be glad to know that the place where we eventually will be has no malaria or typhus, so that is favorable. It is extremely hot around here and sometimes gets way above 100, but cools off at night. Last night a delightful breeze blew in from the ocean and we all slept under blankets.

The girls here all drive their own jeeps and go out on clubmobile runs. Restrictions are few and it certainly makes for a better feeling all the way round.

I shall write my second impression very soon. I still regret not being there for the wedding.

All my love,
Marcia

Marcia Ward Behr

[Biak]
Oct. 11, 1944

Dearest Family,

    I must write in pencil because my pen leaks so. I gave Jim my very best one which someone had given me. I do not begrudge it but wish I had a good one.

    Yesterday Charlie and I and another girl went in three jeeps to visit some troops quite out of the way and far down the line. It was a long drive and we had a man in one of the jeeps for protection. We took some bug juice (lemonade) and the soldiers were very appreciative. I suppose they had not talked to girls since they left Australia over a year ago. It has been mostly combat ever since. The main topic of conversation is "Where do you come from?" and "How long have you been over?" and "You volunteered for this???" It is hard for most men to understand why we wanted to leave home for New Guinea.

    We stayed there for lunch and afterwards visited a native village. Charlie and I rode with two men in one jeep. As we drove along the soldiers pointed out to us the huge impregnable caves where the Japs lived and were in hiding. It is enough just to see them. I certainly don't want to go into them, although they would have taken us. I can imagine how horrible they would be inside. Bones, filth, etc. All the souvenirs would be gone by now. The Japs still come out of the hills on the island. The other day two were caught standing in a chow line. They hid and lived in these caves. They let our men get nicely and safely on the beach and then, when the Americans advanced, there they were in the caves and it took forever to get them out and we lost lots of men.

    The road into the village was so bumpy, great rocks to crawl over, nothing but a jeep could possibly get through. We stopped the jeep just outside the village and the little, almost naked children swarmed around us like flies, chattering and laughing and clapping their hands. They kept saluting us and saying "Hello." It made us laugh and the more we laughed the more excited they became. Some of the youngsters' teeth were beautifully even and white and some, still under ten, had black teeth from chewing betel nuts. Practically everyone over twelve has black teeth and very red gums and tongues from these nuts.

    We all got out of the jeep and their enthusiasm increased. We walked along into the village. Out from the water — many of the houses are on stilts in the water — and out of the thatched houses and out from behind trees, came more and more little black people — old and young, men and women — some with G.I. clothes — some with just G-strings. All of them were shouting and laughing and saluting. I didn't want to look around too much — that is, not to attract any more attention because I had the feeling that with a little encouragement they would have been all over us.

COFFEE and SYMPATHY
World War II Letters from the Southwest Pacific

I turned around and such a reception I have never seen. We were "white queens." It was almost frightening and yet very funny. They wanted to touch us. I remember one woman, with wild hair and big wide black teeth and dark red gums, walking beside me, and just "beating her chops" in her native tongue and holding her hand up quite near me. She wanted to touch us but did not quite dare, for which I was thankful as I was not too sure of their cleanliness. I thought then that a missionary's work could be inspiring. We were really glad to get back to our jeep because everyone had reached such a pitch of hysteria that any more would have led to a riot. Many little ones ran after us as puppies run barking after cars. It was an experience I shall never forget.

Two nights in a row we have had air raid alerts. We aroused ourselves about 3 a.m. and parked on blankets out in front of the foxholes. The first night I rather anticipated a bombing experience. I have heard so much about it. I have vicariously experienced it, but sitting there waiting I wondered if I would be terribly frightened. Some of the girls on the nearby island had been through a couple of raids a months ago, but Charlie and I never had. Of course nothing happened. They bombed some place near us. The next night the same thing.

I am so glad I came up here before going home. This place is at the end of a hot period of the war and so I have been able to realize and appreciate the war activity though still vicariously. I am sure I prefer it that way. Then, too, the terrain here is slightly different from New Guinea — nearer the equator, practically on it, and the most beautiful sunsets I have ever seen. Each one is entirely different and equally vivid. Some shades and colors and combinations of colors that I do not even remember being part of the rainbow. Speaking of rainbows, I have seen them in a complete circle here.

I would not say that the island is pretty. It is interesting geologically being all coral and once sunken, so they say. The elements are the most intriguing. It is not too hot at all and every night I pull up the blanket. Every few weeks we get terrific winds, not treacherous, but quite strong. It sunshines much more often than it rains, but it pours enough to keep down the coral dust which makes your hair gray after a short jeep ride, and to keep the greenage ever green and the land wet. Water is plentiful but yellow. We have been doing all our own washing including boiling our sheets on an army field range in a G.I. can. Everything that was white is now yellow.

Probably, when you get this letter Sylvia and Jack will be married. I shall not miss another family wedding.

                                                Much love to all
                                                Marcia

Marcia Ward Behr

[Biak]
Oct. 19, 1944

Dearest Family,

    I had a letter from Jim today, written a month ago just after I had seen him. It was sent to my old address. There is no doubt about it but the mail has been at fault. I am so relieved and happy. I am just going to trust in God and Jim from now on. He does want me to go home, "But, Marcia, I do want you to go home and give up this sort of climate and life. It's just no good and is apt to ruin your health. It's hard to notice a rapid change due to the slow evolution. I really would like to insist upon this, dear, and hope that you will carry it through."
    I know that he must have written much more and perhaps has not received many of mine. We certainly have trouble and I should not have worried but I guess I am only human.
    So far this overseas experience has been good but staying longer will only tire me. The spontaneity will be gone. I am trying to use reason and do the right thing. Something presses me to go home and, of course, Jim wants me to leave. The Red Cross girls here [Biak] are pleasant and that is great. We do some very exciting and glamorous things besides our Jeep-canteen work. We go boating — hopping to different locales for dinner and some flying but I also state that the best men I met were at Cairns and a few in Brisbane.
    The desire to go on in the hopes of seeing bigger and better lands is not strong enough to urge me to stay. I am going home. Talking to other people makes me vacillate, so, this time I shall take the step without discussion.

                                                   Much love,
                                                   Marcia

[Biak]
Nov. 11, 1944

Dearest Family now enlarged,

    As you can gather I am still here and have not heard from my resignation. It is now ll p.m. and I have been trying all day to find peace and quiet to write. Our new living area and quarters are luxurious but even less private than the other place. There is no guard during the day and hence a steady stream of callers all the time. Mostly people you hope you will never see again. Then we have only had electricity in the tents since yesterday. I had promised to go to an officers' club opening and so could not write last night.

I have been up and down in moods also and so the whole month has gone by and I know you are waiting to hear or expecting a call from San Francisco. Let me tell you now that it may take me a long time to get home. Transportation is a funny thing. I may even see the Philippines. Some disturbing news is that I heard by direct messenger that Jim's outfit has moved. That explains no letters but leaves me in the dark as to his whereabouts or activities.

Mum, your letters describing the wedding were beautiful and I am going to save them to give to Sylvia. How I would have loved being there. It is hard to believe all the happenings so unforetold two years ago.

We have been waiting for our commissary to be completed. Meanwhile we were having sandwiches flown to us every day from another Red Cross installation on a nearby island.

In our new area we have about two acres or so along the beach just off the main road. Since we were the first women up here and since we were here to see that we got decent quarters, we got them. We picked out a lovely area and scrounged the necessary materials and so we have a luxurious living arrangement.

There are six pyramidal tents all facing the water. Each has a little porch. Now we are three to a tent. We know there will soon be four of us. Our tent sits on a bluff and faces the water away from the afternoon sun but we can still see the sunsets by looking that way. All of us worked diligently to make our own places attractive and comfortable. Ours ended up looking like a circus. We have a white-cotton-parachute ceiling and red cotton bedspreads, a big built-in closet painted yellow with red curtains and a green burlap door (material I bought in Brisbane). We painted our porch chairs cream and red. So, you see, my dears, all is luxurious in this land of heat, mire and jungles.

Tomorrow I am going by boat and plane to an island where there is a civilized village and I am going to stay overnight. Five of us are going with some Navy boys, all very proper you may be sure because we shall be the Mayor's guests. I am very excited about it.

Tonight a friend of Charlie's came for dinner and we had it in our little tent. He brought it all, including the stove. We had western sandwiches, a salad of cucumber, tomato, lettuce, radishes, onions — all transported from Cairns, I am sure. We also had maple sugar sent from the U.S.A. Do not think we eat fresh vegetables always. It is usually canned cabbage or silver beet tops (kuni grass) sent from Australia and bully beef. However, my weight has not changed.

                                             All my love,
                                             Marcia

Marcia Ward Behr

[Biak]
Nov. 18, 1944

My Dearest Family,

I am on top of the world today. I knew I brought the script of *Sparkin'* for a good cause and now, at the last gasp of my overseas career, I pulled it out of the bottom of my footlocker, and last night, after three days of rehearsal, we gave the first performance to an audience of 1,500 G.I.s and they loved it. I really can say I gave my best performance ever of Granny. It had many new colors because I was so chuckling and happy inside from the very first when I said, "Well, if she ain't, you better take her into Doc Spelzer's and have her 'zamined. There must be something wrong with her somewhurs." You remember that is after Lessie says she "ain't thinkin' about no fellers?"

Special Services came over Monday and asked for some girls to help out in a variety show they were rehearsing. I talked to the man and got two other girls. We read the skit they had and decided it was no good. I threw in a suggestion about *Sparkin'*. They accepted it and the rest was up to me: to find a boy, get a mother — I had the girl to play the daughter, to rehearse it and organize the props and costumes. Well, we did it and you can really be proud of me this time, if I do say so as I should not. Now, I know for sure I still have the old spark in me yet.

But, honestly, is life not full of the most wonderful surprises, if we just hang in there long enough? Honestly, I get so darn depressed and this time I had been down for a good long time. Momentary risings, yes, but it has been months and months since I have really been as high as I am now. Not since my great correspondence with Jim and hopes of seeing him and getting to know him were imminent.

Though I have not heard anything from him since that last letter, my faith has not wavered. No one ever had so much faith in a man under such trying circumstances. Maybe I am crazy. Oh well, I might just as well be faithful.

"Granny" certainly is a hit. No sense being modest about it. It is true and the second night I was better than the first, though I was more nervous beforehand. Now we shall play it almost every night until we cover all the troops. It is really something to play before such vast audiences every night. One colonel kept calling me Helen Hayes afterwards. I really am funny and you know how good that script is and the characters are familiar to all the boys. "Lessie" and "Orry" are very cute and very good too.

It just shows that, if you do a good job of something and it is comedy, the G.I.s will accept it. I do not think a play has ever been done up here before. Short vaudeville skits, maybe, but never anything with characters and *Sparkin'* is just perfect.

Yesterday Lt. Jack Baird and Lt. Hoover, Navy friends from Cairns, had planned to take me and the three other tentmates on a boat ride to collect shells on some of the small islands around. They had to come quite a distance to get us. Well, they did not come. Luckily we had parked our jeep with some Dutchmen who knew Jack Baird. They took us in and treated us royally all day. They gave us a wonderful Javanese dinner "mit" rice and everything. Then they took us to an interesting native village. We did get some shells after all.

A message came from Jack Baird that they were bringing the picnic things over to us by the regular boat at four o'clock. So we had our picnic dinner with them at our tent.

I met a Javanese colonel who had lectured at Bennington — most cultured. He showed Javanese dances there and he knew Martha Hill and the Fergussons and stayed with the McCulloughs. It was just an "old home week." He had lectured at 30 other colleges and, funny, but the other one he mentioned was Wells [where my sisters went]. He is a lecturer on Eastern civilization and culture. His name is Raden Abdulkadir. Do you remember him, Nan or Syl? He taught me some Malay and now I can speak a few words to our Javanese laundress. Are we not ritzy to have our laundry done? She is so sweet and so tiny. Her name is Wilder Nung.

All my love,
Marcia

[Biak]
Nov. 23, 1944

Dearest Family,

Happy Thanksgiving. How I would like to be home now and I really mean that with all my heart. I am supposed to wait 60 days for my resignation to go through. It has been over a month now so I may get home by February. It is all very indefinite; expect me when you see me or I will call from San Francisco.

I suppose we all have had at least ten turkey dinner invitations.

Mary Ellen, one of our tentmates, and I are going for one o'clock lunch to an officers' mess. I expect it will be good because they have "fatcats" going to Australia all the time. Fatcats are planes used for food and liquor supplies. The invitation is for all afternoon and evening. — an orchestra and a flow of beer, so they say. However, I am planning to go to a Navy mess for dinner with Charlie, so I hope to get away from the earlier event in time.

Mary Ellen, who plays the mother in *Sparkin'* and sings in the show, made herself a beautiful evening dress out of a salvaged silk parachute. She got it from the same boys who gave Marge Shirley, our other tentmate, and me each a whole silk parachute. In appreciation we gave the boys a date. Nice people, aren't we? We told them it would be best to have a picnic supper at our tent. We are on the water and the porch is quite adequate for entertaining. It is very attractive with the furniture we painted red and white and three fern plants.

We also told our dates we could not procure the food, so they did. They brought twelve beautiful T-bone steaks, potatoes, onions, oranges, beer, ice, everything! The dinner was marvelous but they were hard to handle afterwards. They asked us to come to their mess hall for turkey sandwiches and we did and it was a mistake. The turkey was great but after that they drove us all around with one thing on their minds. Mine was the nicest. He was a college graduate.

I did not have much trouble but I gather the others had quite a time. Finally, they brought us home but after curfew. We are now restricted and we are all so happy about it. We asked Mandy, the boss, to make it for two weeks instead of three days. Now we have a marvelous excuse and no one can bother us at night for all that time.

I still must write to Syl and Jack. I received a letter today with her engagement picture. I am dying to see pictures of the wedding.

Not another letter from Jim and I still do not know where he is. Thank goodness, I have the play to keep my mind occupied. People roar at me and whistle and applaud at the end of the Granny act. It seems like an ovation. It is good that I make so many men laugh. I am glad I can do it.

I must get ready to go to turkey dinner now.

All my love,
Marcia

[Biak]
Nov. 25, 1944

Dearest Family,

Nothing new, except more performances of the play. You can be proud of me, of that I assure you. Helen Barrie, A.R.C., who works at a division club where we played last Tuesday, quoted one boy. He does not read or write too well. He said he wanted Helen to tell me that he thought "I was best of all and that I was the prettiest too." The colored officers performing on the same show call me "The Old Trouper." I appreciate their approval because they are no slouches and are really liked by the audiences. They are all top-notch professionals in civilian life.

I sent some snaps in my last letter. We are taking some of our tent and when they are developed, I shall send you one.

There is talk of a tour of the islands with the show but I want to come home. No word from Jim. I keep on writing. I shall until he says something. He may be sick or he may be in Leyte, I don't know.

I am doing pretty well in making the Javanese girl, who does our washing, understand me. She brings different members of her family with her every day. Today there are one young girl and two small children. I asked the girl what they call the doll she was holding. It is "baby" or some such sounding name.

We had a wonderful Thanksgiving yesterday at the officers' club. It is an attractive place right on the water — a long porch and inside was brightly decorated with yellow and blue parachutes with lamp shades made from the noses of P38s (fighter planes). Two orchestras played all afternoon and evening — tap dancers and singers and, of course, a bit of beer. It was quite fancy for the jungles. My date was very pleasant, at least he was handsome, not thrilling, but no strain. That's what counts.

All my love,
Marcia

[Biak]
Nov. 27, 1944

Dearest Family,

Nightly now I gradually transform myself into old Granny Sparks. I put the cotton on my chin and on each eyebrow and smooth the makeup over my face, working in the shadowing and painting with the liner. My cotton dress is just right and my felt Aussie slippers are comfortably sloppy looking. My homemade wee wire specs are just the perfect touch. The nightly crowd keeps increasing. We have now given six performances and appeared before nearly 30,000 people.

I am becoming mike-conscious and feel quite at home on a truck-trailer stage playing out under the stars. The G.I.s like *Sparkin'*. They really do. It just goes to show that, if it is the right material, it goes over. The play is not risqué; it is homespun, familiar characters and situations, not a wasted word in the script — it is alive! And they laugh!

One begins to take matters for granted so much, that I hardly realize how thrilling this really is for me. To glow inside and know that the audience feels it and that we are giving so many people laughter, is the most wonderful thing to me. Yet I am really in my right place. It is the thing I do best and I should be doing it. So my ego is not inflated and it just seems like part of my overseas job — just another phase. I went out and served juice today and the boys were so appreciative. The reaction to the juice was the same as the nightly applause. It is something really tangible that I am passing out because, at the time, I possess it, whether it is laughs or lemonade.

You know, too, though I do not hear from Jim, I feel happy all the same. I write and tell him all and I believe that he must get my letters and he would write if he could and he must love me. So I keep on. There is no one else, so I love him. I meet other people, lots of other people, but there is always Jim. Something is bound to happen to prove me wrong or right. In the meantime I go on. I just don't write when I feel low. I am obsessed and that is all there is to it.

We all gave our best show last night and I am so glad. It was at a huge general hospital. It seems that each stage gets worse. It's most important that we are heard and moving about and using mikes takes manipulating. Last night they told us that it was a trailer stage and a truck for a dressing room. There were only two directional mikes (you can only be heard when standing right in front and close to them). Well, we arrived. There was the audience and the barren stage under the stars. I looked at the dim lights hanging overhead and just sighed with faint hope of being seen or heard.

I began the makeup process in full view of the waiting audience. (The boys usually gather an hour or so ahead of time.) I could hardly see what I was doing. Someone held up a flashlight for me. I kept wondering what was the use? The soldier who played Orry was most depressed. He said, "This might as well be our last if lights and mikes are going to be like this." I didn't say anything. I was just concentrating on getting into makeup and costume. Mary Ellen was inside the truck and she had put on her beautiful white silk parachute evening dress for her singing act before she changed to play Ma in *Sparkin'*. She must have stood on her head to do it. I crawled into the truck to finish dressing. Mary Ellen said "I feel that it will be good tonight" and deep down inside I felt so too. I said, "It certainly isn't the audience's fault that the facilities are bad, and we will manage somehow." I felt calmly nervous. I was all dressed and ready before the beginning of the show. The M.C. sounded ten thousand times better than ever.

The audience was immediately responsive and warm. We all felt better and my makeup was very good. We all said, "Let's have fun!"

We walked on the bare platform, took our places. I heard a few laughs and some comments. I looked out into the sea of faces and grinned. I felt safe. We began. They were with us from the first sentence: "Is Tude gone to bed, Suzy?" says Granny. I was determined to be heard and it was part of Granny's character. I turned the mike toward me when I spoke and turned it back to Ma. I tried to time my walks so I would hit the other mike to speak. I raised my voice in the center. Orry and Lessie tried to do the same and, by gum, they heard every word. Everyone said it was the best performance and I think it was the very best Granny I have ever performed. So you see, hardships and it is so exciting! It is a job and I love to do it.

We have been asked to go to two nearby islands. Transportation will be by air and fast boat. Maybe we can tour other places. Otherwise, I am awaiting my travel orders. What is to be will be.

I am so glad to write this happy letter.

> All my love,
> Marcia

[Biak]
Nov. 28, 1944

Dearest Family,

Last night's audience was the most amazing of all. It was a colored infantry outfit from which the Negro orchestra comes and they asked us to give the show there. Any ovation in any theatre in the world would be tame compared to the reception the whole show received last night. Even the stars were jumping with their shouts, laughter and whistles.

The Negro lieutenants told Mary Ellen that, when the men heard that four A.R.C. girls were to be in the show, they started sitting on the ground in front of the stage at 5 p.m. and the show began at 7:00. Just as we were about to begin, the mike went on the bum. We waited and finally they managed to get hold of an Aussie mike — not too good. Again we had a bare stage with all sides open but a roof over the top and a dressing room. This time we even had the audience behind us. I felt like an actor of the Italian Commedia dell' Arte.

We walked on the stage in character and took our places. This audience started laughing right away. We were leery of them; even the lieutenant in the show from the outfit was not too sure of the reception. If they do not like you, they just sit and nothing can arouse them or they might even stone us, as they did the last show. So, you see, we take our lives in our hands.

This time we had to play entirely into the mikes. I used the fullest voice and you know that can be loud. The huge audience really cheered us at the end and the laughs were terrific throughout. I would like to write to Mr. Conkle, the author, and let him know what a great and universal play *Sparkin'* is and let him in on its reception.

We have been invited to play a Navy base. This means an overnight trip. I doubt very much if we can take the review on an extended tour as the Special Services have been hoping. There are too many people involved and much too much red tape to get the performers released from their outfits. There is not a dead act in the show. It is very professional. In fact, Mary Ellen said that, after we played the hospital, people with theatre background and many others streamed into the A.R.C. club there (M.E. is doing detached service with the hospital during the day) and raved about the show. They said it was better than any they have seen over here — barring none.

I do not know what is happening to my homecoming. The area director is away but, when he returns, I shall ask him to hurry my travel orders.

I have some pictures of the show, not too good but interesting. We have one shot of the audience taken during the performance in the pouring rain. I shall bring them home with me.

My love to the whole family,
Marcia

[Biak]
Dec. 8, 1944

Dear Mom and All,

It is too terrible about Roger. I just can't believe it. Poor Cece and her little baby girl. And Roger had just gotten his Navy wings and to go down on a routine flight over Pensacola is so sad. My unhappiness, if any, certainly has no justification and I have no right to complain about anything. I shall write Cece.

I found out that Jim is in forward areas. I should simply forget him. I cannot expect a man to hang on to such a flimsy issue for so long. I can do it but, then, I am just one of those stick-to-it people. My mind is hard to change once I feel it is right. I am glad to be coming home now. The A.R.C. cannot give me any definite time of departure. Christmas is certainly out but it may be soon after that or it could be spring. I am coming and I am very happy about it.

All my love,
Marcia

[Biak]
Dec. 17, 1944

Dearest Family,

I am most depressed that there is no hope of my getting home for Christmas. In fact, it is best that you do not expect me until you see me. My chances of flying are out. I see that now. Too many wounded are being evacuated these days for me to take up room. I shall just have to wait my turn patiently and hope that one day soon I shall have a sack on an eastward-bound ship.

It is the most heavenly day — a sea breeze floats into our tent and makes it difficult to manage this paper but any wind is such a relief to the heat that we do not care if all our laundry blows off the line. In fact, I just finished washing my two sheets and all my towels and I expect they are on the ground by now.

Barbara Rosenthal's brother was visiting her here in Biak and so she wanted to take him to Japen Island where there is a real village. I had flown over it once but you have to go by boat or seaplane to stop there. We did not know anyone at the seaplane base, and it is a 90-mile trip by boat, so the former is the most practical means of travel. Barbara trotted herself over to operations the other day and found that someone was going and would take us with them. Barbara and I, her brother and another girl went over the day before yesterday. At operations we met the pilot, a very attractive captain. I was so excited and happy to be going on this trip because all our other plans to go there had fallen through. I thought I would just never get to the island of Japen.

We flew over the water and looked down on the native homes built out over the water. Then, after flying about an hour, you suddenly look down on a very pretty little harbor. From the air you see streets and houses, farmlands stretching from the water's edge to the foot of the verdant hills. It would be about the only spot for this village because the rest of the island is hilly right down to the shoreline.

We circled around and finally made the water landing. Pretty soon a lieutenant of the Dutch government came out with two natives in a little boat with an outboard motor. The islanders are always pleased to have visitors and greeted us with smiles and handshakes. Our captain-pilot had been over a few days before so he made the introductions.

I cannot tell you how excited we were to be in this "out-of-the-world" civilization. The stone jetty appeared to be of a certain age and later I asked the lieutenant about the age of the settlement and he said Dutch missionaries came around the beginning of this century.

There was some strafing damage but this was mostly evident in the clipped-off coconut palms. I was struck with the happiness of the whole village. They do all the farming by hand and in a short time have built an irrigation system which equals that of any built by bulldozers and such modern contraptions. Red and pale yellow hibiscus crawl up and down the wooden fences in front of the frame houses. The architecture is simple — designed for tropical comfort. Oriental touches, certainly not elaborate, lend enough atmosphere for the tourists' artistic satisfaction. The houses are of two story height, with wide doorways and plenty of windows in most of them. Some of the roofs are thatched with dried palm leaves and some are just wooden. I noticed that a few houses seemed to be made out of stucco.

We tramped all through the village. I could not help exclaiming about the flowers, cut lawns, fruit trees and small vegetable gardens. Here was civilization again and I felt a definite foreign atmosphere and culture, though minute, that I hardly found at all in Australia. In Cairns there was some because of the many Chinese, Italians and Hindus. The Hindus were imported as laborers to work in the sugarcane fields, but they lent a cosmopolitan air as they mingled with the various Cairnsites on the main streets. They were always barefooted and turbaned and they generally wore western civilian trousers. I don't remember ever seeing any Hindu women in Cairns.

The streets of the village on Japen were really wide graveled footpaths lined by palms or other tropical trees. The main village on the harbor is inhabited by Chinese as well as Javanese. Then you walk another mile to the Papuan native village. It is tidier and cleaner than the ones I visited in New Guinea.

I walked ahead with the captain-pilot. In conversation he said his home was Utica, New York. I asked him if he knew the Owens. He did. Then I asked him about Muffy Sicard and he knew Muffy very well. Naturally, I told him that she is now a member of our family. He nearly died and said, "Your brother is Tom Ward — well, they were married in our backyard!"

The surprise element is always present. You walk beside strangers and suddenly there springs up a bond that was there but dormant. The trip became secondary for awhile as we talked of home and friends in common. He has not met Tom and was not at the wedding. You, Mother and Daddy, may have stayed at Marshall Shantz's home. That is the captain's name by the way. He is now married and lives in Jamesport, New York. He started out on an acting career but ended up in radio, found it a better means of livelihood. He is certainly nice and about the most gentlemanly person I have met in the New Guinea area. We walked through the freshly transplanted rice fields where a number of natives toiled in the hot sun. It was dreadfully warm and we walked more than I have for many months. We are not able to walk anywhere except in our compound. It would be a little conspicuous with the many troops about and no civilians. Anyway, there is nowhere to walk except in jungles or swamps or dusty coral roads. So we did enjoy a long stroll in the pastoral fields of the island.

We came back to the Dutch officer's residence and were served coconut juice on their stone porch by a Javanese girl dressed in a sarong. This is not the Hollywood variety but a long piece of hand-dyed material wrapped straight around the hips and hanging nearly to the bare ankles. A tight, long-sleeved waist is worn over the sarong and is hip length. As we were sitting there, an officer drove up in the town's only jeep, acquired just the day before. He had jammed it full of little dark children, all laughing and shouting with glee. They had been driving all over the village and having the time of their lives. The children came up and wanted to sing for us much to our pleasure. They sang several Dutch numbers, one Javanese song and Pistol Packin' Mama and She'll Be Coming Round the Mountain. It was lots of fun and they were so adorable. We gave them each a package of Lifesavers and they went running to tell other children and share their candy.

It was 4:30 and so we said our goodbyes, etc. and got in the little motor boat. It did not run any more, so three natives grabbed the oars and, in spite of a dead motor, we reached the seaplane quite speedily and took off for Biak.

I cannot seem to speed my travel orders. There is an A.R.C. rule that you must wait 60 days after resigning — I suppose that is to see if you change your mind. I have not changed mine. I am sure it is the right thing for me to do, though I may regret not waiting to see the Philippines. Enough is enough and I can always recall the reasons for my decision, which, I may add, were not prompted by Jim's advice alone. Though I do not hear from him, my decision remains the same and I am not depressed about him either. What is to be will be and I shall keep the large perspective of things. Time will tell.

Merry Christmas everyone,

Love,
Marcia

Marcia Ward Behr

[Biak]
Dec. 18, 1944

Dear Tom and Muffy,

Merry Christmas and a Happy New Year. Gosh, I wish I could get home in time for Christmas and the birth of your little one, but I won't even be on my way. There is a 60-day wait after resignation and I cannot seem to buck it in any way. If I could get some flying orders, it would be great, but that is very unlikely.

Many people returning from the States say they are glad to be out here — that back there everyone speaks a different language. Naturally, some people there cannot visualize the war out here. It is quite different from Europe and I imagine people do talk more about the Allies' advance into France and feel that part of the war coming to an end.

At any rate, I am prepared in my mind for life at home and I do not expect to be restless. Sometimes I may wish to be out here in the excitement, but it is not exciting daily, it is only in the sum total that the adventure lies. It is how one reacts to events that is important. Something will turn up for me to do at home, I am sure.

Marshall Schantz is certainly a nice person, Muffy. I nearly died when he said the wedding was at his home. He took me up in a Cub plane yesterday and he looped it around and around. The world looks just the same upside down. My hands became instantly cold but no other reaction. I am now back in the routine job of jeep-mobile-canteens. The play is over but it was lots of fun while it lasted and the boys really liked us.

We have had some pictures taken of our tent and surroundings which I shall bring home with me. I shall be seeing you in another month or two.

All my love,
Marcia

[Biak]
December 22, 1944

Dearest Family,

I realize now I should never have excited you about my early return but I really did not know it would take so long to get out of here. However, I am coming. I still feel it is the right thing to do. I am yearning to see my family again.

Dec. 27, 1944

One thing and another has kept me from completing this letter. As a matter of fact, there are four of us living in this tent and one table in the middle of the floor. There are always people around and we all treasure any moments when we can concentrate long enough to write a letter.

I now have my travel orders. A sailing date is still unknown. I shall just have "to sweat that out." I shall probably get home just in time to be appalled by the spring fashions. It will be wonderful to dress like a woman again.

I think I shall just skip telling you about Christmas. It was not much fun. We all felt the same way. Christmas night we went to see *Saratoga Trunk* at the Special Services camp where we spent our time during the tour of the show. (We worked with these servicemen. The show had nothing to do with the U.S.O.) The movie was simply excellent. Do not miss it. I have now seen it twice. I never used to go to the movies at all but Marshall Schantz comes and takes us all. He is a good escort and they are sadly lacking around here. Amazing, but true.

Marshall was in the Philippines for Christmas and found his brother there. He came back yesterday but will soon be leaving for good.

Tomorrow is my day off and I plan to wash and iron everything and pack. I am leaving for A.P.O. 560 [Hollandia, a base on Dutch New Guinea] on Monday because more ships sail for the States from there. I cannot get air priority because I am not sick and there is no emergency. However, now that I have missed Christmas, I might just as well relax and wait for my ship. It will be a good rest and I can finish a sweater I started in Brisbane.

I have just finished making sandwiches all morning and this afternoon and there is a definite aroma of peanut butter and salmon spread about me that a cold shower will remove.

It is never too terribly hot here but perhaps I am just getting used to it. I imagine the cold weather in New York will be a terrific shock to me.

All my love,
Marcia

Marcia Ward Behr

[Hollandia]
Jan. 3, 1945

Dearest Family,

I am waiting now in A.P.O. 565 for my ship. I should not be here much more than a week.

I heard some very good news today about Jim. He left here for the States a week ago. His ship was blown up and he escaped without a scratch. Of course, I have heard no word from him. He may think I have gone home. In case he calls me, do tell him I shall be home within the month.

I am dreadfully tired. This morning I flew from Biak to Hollandia in New Guinea and had to hitchhike 30 miles to the base in order to speak to someone about transportation. The A.R.C. would have let me rot in 920 [Biak], I guess, unless I had come down here on my own to get transportation on a ship.

If I had not bumped into a Red Cross girl who knew Jim, I would not know what had happened to him. On the other hand, it is bad to hear about him because it stirs me up again and I have been very good about adjusting myself to the unsolved mystery about Jim Wilder. He must be very tired and I am so glad that he is going home at last for a much needed rest.

It is so exciting about Junior and I am so impressed with being an aunt and having children in the family again. I love little babies and I can hardly wait to see my little nephew, Tom Sedgwick Ward, Jr. I am so happy both mother and child are well.

All my love,
Marcia

P.S. I shall be very impatient waiting here for the ship.

[Hawaii]
Jan. 12, 1945

Dearest Family,

As you can see I am accomplishing something that seemed utterly out of my reach. A miracle happened and here I am at the Moana Hotel in Honolulu. I left Holandia the day before yesterday. I told you the news I heard about Jim and that he was on his way home after losing his ship in a battle near the Philippines. I wanted so much to be home in case he called me. I brooded about it for several days and made an attempt to fly from 565 [Hollandia] to the States. It was hopeless. Orders to fly are only given to the brass, the sick and wounded, or for a real emergency case. I had already been at the embarkation point [Hollandia] a week. There would eventually be space on a troop ship but the planes were needed to fight the war in the Pacific.

A Red Cross girl suggested I try to hitchhike plane rides to San Francisco. The suggestion seemed preposterous. I was warned that if I were caught midway without proper orders to fly, the Red Cross would send me back to Brisbane to wait for a troop ship and that could be a two-months delay. Then I heard a rumor that the troop ship in 565 [Hollandia], that I would be taking, was going down to Australia first and this crushed me completely. Jim would be gone again and no hope at all for me to see him.

I got into bed and tossed. I wanted to get home quickly. I simply had to fly. That was all there was to it. I got out of bed and re-packed everything, making my baggage as light as possible and asked the M.P. to awaken me early, so that I could go before dawn with the Red Cross canteen girls to the airstrip. I decided that if I did succeed in getting a ride anywhere, I would fly the rest of the way somehow. I knew it meant much strain, fast talking and perhaps shedding a few tears, but the urge was strong enough and I was determined to make the attempt.

I started to go to Operations at the airport, but changed my mind, deciding that would be the wrong approach. Using proper channels was out. Then I heard that some Navy planes were taking off that morning. I went out on the tarmac to wait for the pilots. I sat down on my duffle bag and waited nearly three hours. Finally, two Navy pilots came. They said they were going to Manus in the Admiralty Islands and they would be happy to take me. It was not a transport plane. So that was easy and I calmed down inside. Little did I realize that these islands were only a stone's throw from 565 [Hollandia] and just north of eastern New Guinea. On my way at last I felt confident that the first step would be the hardest.

The nice nurses at Manus gave me a bed for the night and one wonderful nurse studied the only copy of a travel order the Army had given me. It was meant to fly me as far as Hollandia to secure ship passage to the United States. The nurse exclaimed, "Why, this is written in such a way that you can use it to take you by air all the way to the States. The problem is you should really have seven copies, so that you can leave a copy at each base where you land."

The clever nurse arranged for me to fly the next morning to Honolulu by way of Kwajalein and Johnston islands! I chose to visit Honolulu for two days and the first night I enjoyed my first tub-bath in almost two years. It is hard to believe that I am here and that the famous Waikiki Beach is the view from my hotel window. The war has made a great difference here — so many people and not the same care and attention to upkeep and improvements and, of course, the labor shortages. It all reminds me of Brisbane.

I really hope to leave today. The Navy has arranged for me to be the first woman to fly in one of the huge flying boats built by Howard Hughes. We will arrive in Los Angeles tomorrow morning.

I am anxious to get on to the States. I keep thinking about my family and how glad we will be to see each other. Of course, Honolulu is fun and still exciting. It impresses people that I look so well. They can be reassured that no harm comes to women living in the jungles. They expect to see a living yellow skeleton, dried up and jungle-rotted. Men in Honolulu who have been out in the Pacific War Area especially comment on the fact that I look as though I had just left the States instead of 21 months ago.

I have to go now and shall try to finish this letter in Los Angeles.

All my love,
Marcia

Homecoming

I never added to that letter. From Los Angeles it took two days and three different planes for me to reach Columbus, Ohio, where the last of my three pilots was forced down in a blinding snowstorm. But I was lucky; I caught a 10 p.m. train for Washington, D. C. Then, on January 16, 1945, I surrendered my G. I. equipment — helmet, gas mask, canteen, knapsack — to the Army, and the Red Cross gave me an official letter of commendation.

A day later, we had a very joyful family reunion in New York, and I met a baby nephew and a new brother-in-law. A few days later I called Jim Wilder's home. His mother answered the phone. "Is Jim there?" I asked. "Why, no, we have not heard anything from our son for over a month." I said, "I am Marcia Ward, a friend of Jim. He is on his way home. His ship was destroyed in a battle. He was not hurt at all and is coming home on leave."

Mrs. Wilder was so happy to hear the report of Jim — she invited me to come to dinner. I was an angel bringing heavenly news. I think the Wilders were concerned about Jim and his sister both being divorced. She remarked wistfully, "They are probably too good-looking." Of course, their children were handsome. Both parents were well built with even features and sparkling blue eyes. Mr. Wilder's captivating smile made me feel close to his son. It was a very pleasant evening and Mrs. Wilder said that Jim would call me.

Jim called me about a week later. He was very handsome in his Navy uniform. We went to see *The Voice of the Turtle* at the old Morosco theater. Quite a risqué play for 1945. Afterwards, in the taxi on the way to my parents' apartment, I remember that Jim enfolded me in his arms, and later on the large comfortable sofa in their living room we sat kissing and talking until very late. He had seemed nervous and keyed up all evening. I thought this was understandable after his suffering through a battle and losing his ship. Then, that night he told me that there was a nurse, named Eleanor, whom he knew in Milne Bay. At that moment she was trying to get passage from the South Pacific to New York. Finally, he admitted that he had become very "involved" with her and had bought a ring in Los Angeles that his sister, who lived there, was to give Eleanor when she disembarked.

What did this mean? It was unbelievable! I felt an emotional implosion but I couldn't cry. Why hadn't he told me earlier? He tried to explain how their relationship developed. I sensed that, having seen me again, he was now torn between us. I don't remember reproaching him for his "unfaithfulness," although he surely should have written me about the situation.

Two years overseas in the war certainly had its effect on both of us. Because I felt at loose ends, needing the anchor of friendship and work, I was unwilling to let Jim go. Meanwhile, he seemed tense and confused and was drinking too much. My brother-in-law, who was no saint, observed that Jim could really absorb the booze.

Perhaps, when Jim saw me in Milne Bay that time, I did not measure up to his memory of me on the beach at Yorkies Knob. So I wondered. Instead of a pleasant hour's visit, we had experienced a rushed ten minutes together before I had to fly back to Oro Bay. However, that was hardly sufficient reason for breaking up a nine-month serious relationship. But Jim couldn't seem to explain why he hadn't told me the truth.

Nevertheless, we did see each other in New York for over two months. Jim and I often frequented the little bar at the Hotel Carlyle and a restaurant called Peter's Backyard in the Village near the hall where I was rehearsing an Equity Library play in which I had a good part. Jim watched rehearsals, we went to movies and plays, and I introduced him to my friends. I gave him the navy blue sweater knitted in Brisbane. I longed to dance with him again, and we were going to the spring concert of the University Glee Club at the Waldorf. Afterwards there would be dancing with a great band. Unfortunately, President Roosevelt died that day and the dance was canceled.

As always, I remained virginal in our warm embraces. Perhaps, we did not really love each other, but there must have been some kind of a bond between us. Nine months of exchanging "love letters" surely had some psychological impact.

Although Jim had told me that the nurse, Eleanor, was seeking passage to the States, I was emotionally unprepared for the news of her arrival. I remember that we had been to dinner and the movies and that we were seated on the same sofa in my parents' apartment, and Jim looked at me and said, "Eleanor has the ring, she is on her way and will be here probably tomorrow."

So, that was the end. I was unable to say anything. Nevertheless, I felt he was reluctant to lose me. He said, "I want to see you again someday." What did that signify? I saw clearly the future without Jim. I think I told him as much with my long questioning look. He had never even tried to give up Eleanor. What was her hold on him? (Did it occur to me why she was able to get an Army discharge? No. Now I know that Army nurses signed up for the duration of the war, just as the men did. If they married, it was possible to get out, and certainly if a nurse became pregnant, she had to leave the service.) I felt helpless and he offered no other explanation. Perhaps he felt helpless too. The realization of an inevitable outcome strengthened me.

COFFEE and SYMPATHY
World War II Letters from the Southwest Pacific

I wonder now why the tragedy of that final separation from Jim did not tear me apart. No tears, no pleading words, I simply remember saying, "I'll be all right." The actress in me must have known "how to express the hidden torment" that at last released me from a long emotional entanglement.

A few days later I was lunching at Peter's Backyard with Betsy Drake, the ingenue in the Equity Library play, and Helen Harvey, the director. Jim was there and came over to us, leaving Eleanor seated at a distant table. She was wearing her army uniform, but I could not see her face. Jim reached our table and greeted us with a laugh. I said as gaily as I could, "Hello. What are you doing here?" He answered that he had taken Eleanor to all our spots.

One day after rehearsal, Helen, Betsy and I went to the nearby movies and found Jim alone in the empty balcony. Betsy and Helen moved past Jim leaving the seat next to him for me. I felt shy but asked him where Eleanor was. He told me that Eleanor had gone to her home town to get discharged from the Army. Jim was in uniform and that was the last time I saw him. Is it possible that he had married overseas? I wondered but never found out.

The play, *The Moon and the Yellow River* by Dennis Johnston, opened ten days later in that month of May 1945, and the New York Daily Mirror gave me the first mention, so that was helpful. I kept busy looking for acting and radio soap opera work, with some success in the latter. Finally, a year later, Alfred de Liagre, Jr., a theatrical producer and director, hired me as his girl Friday. It was a glamorous job and, although I was not acting much, at least I was part of the Broadway scene. This was a period of wonderful theater: *A Streetcar Named Desire, South Pacific, The Glass Menagerie, Death of a Salesman* plus *The Madwoman of Chaillot* that de Liagre produced and directed. Although I saw my friends and had dates, it was a lonely time, and I was grateful for theater work.

In the late spring of 1946, I was surprised to receive a call from Mrs. Wilder inviting me to dinner. I remember that we talked generalities through dinner. Afterwards we sat in the living room and Mrs. Wilder came over to me with a picture of a baby boy. No need to tell me whose child it was. I saw a shocking likeness. "He looks just like Jim," I said trying to be enthusiastic. I wondered how old he was, but didn't ask.

I thanked the Wilders for a lovely evening. Mr. Wilder, a charming man with the same smile and eyes that I loved in Jim, escorted me to my Fifth Avenue bus. As we waited he talked about his son, implying that the war had changed him. He said, "It is better for you this way." I wondered what he meant and replied, "It's all right now." I felt that Jim's parents respected me, and it seemed that he was trying to say they were sorry if Jim had caused me any unhappiness. Possibly the father was concerned about his son's future. We shook hands and said goodbye. I looked into his blue eyes while he briefly held my hand. Then I stepped onto the bus and turned to wave goodbye. On the long ride up 5th Avenue I went over and over the evening in my thoughts, but never came to any conclusions, and never heard anything about the Wilders again.

It was three years after that dinner before I saw the real man of my dreams. Ed Behr and I met on a blind date. We fell in love, married and had two great sons. He was truly the man I imagined reading those love letters from New Guinea when I was a Red Cross girl in World War II.

About the Author

Marcia Ward Behr discovered her acting talent in the eighth grade and has never strayed far from the theater. She has been happily married for over fifty years.

She earned a B.A. in drama from Bennington College. Then came summer stock jobs and acting in a repertory company in New York City. Work in a modern dance group led to a vaudeville tour. That was a far cry from roles in Shakespeare, but it paid $25 a week – good money in those Depression years.

Just before Pearl Harbor, Behr received a favorable review in *The New York Times* for her role in a new play, *Escape into Glory*. After the Japanese attack on December 7, 1941, the United States declared war on the fascist countries. Behr soon joined the American Red Cross to work overseas in combat areas and was sent to the recreation clubs in the Southwest Pacific.

After the war, Behr continued her theater career in New York, where she married Ed Behr, a writer for *The Wall Street Journal*. They had two sons, and a few years later the family was transferred to Washington, D.C. Behr acted at the Arena Stage and taught drama at Madeira School and at Sally Smith's Lab School for children with learning disabilities. She developed an acting program for them and published a book about her work.

Marcia Behr and her husband now live in a lifecare community in Maryland, where she directs staged play-readings for the residents. A full house applauds old actors who make the audience believe they are young.

Printed in the United States
6404